Lies My Mind Tells Me

The Secret to Finding Happiness with Anxiety

Tosha McLaren

Cover Art By: Jingyi Wu (<u>Veronnikka</u>) - "Gone"

Dedication

To my sister Brooke. Thank you for being my best friend, my biggest supporter and for "getting me." Thanks for loving me and inspiring me with your great strength.

Table of Contents

Chapter 1

Introduction

Anxiety is not a life sentence.

I wish someone had told me this earlier on in my life. I wish that I had known this when I was a little girl, crying alone on a cold bathroom floor on Christmas Day.

I remember listening to the faint sounds of laughter and festivities in the distance.

I wish that someone had told me that I wouldn't always have to feel this constant darkness.

I wish I knew that it wasn't always going to be like that.

My biggest fear was that this darkness was a permanent, unchanging prison for the rest of my life.

I want you to know that anxiety is not your life sentence.

Mental illness is not a life sentence.

I want you to know that there is so much hope in the world. You have an amazing future in front of you, but only if you're willing to do whatever it takes to heal. I want to be your guide on this road ahead, as I have already walked it. I want to be the one to cure these mental illnesses for you and others. I believe this is my life's mission, and I won't stop until I've achieved everything that I've been placed on this earth to do.

I realized something vitally important: you have to go through times of intense darkness so that you can be the light for someone else. The words that you'll read in this book have all been born out of a life of struggle - the same one you likely face today.

I was diagnosed with OCD when I was only eight years old. The doctor called it the, "youngest and most severe case" he had ever seen. I washed my hands until they bled because I thought it would make me feel calm to be clean. It took me an hour to leave the house because I would walk through the doorway a hundred times back and forth. In my mind, if I didn't do this, my family would surely die. Kids at school occasionally noticed my compulsions, but by nine-years-old I had become masterful at hiding it. Socially, I needed to hide who I truly was, but the internal conflict was deteriorating my body. By the age of 10, I was experiencing intrusive, abusive and sexual thoughts that would torment me. I couldn't engage in activities with the same joy my peers could. I'd stare at the other children during birthday parties as they laughed and pushed each other in the pool with such ease.

I thought to myself, "I want that. I want to be that happy."

Deep down, I never thought I could be. I don't think I'll ever be able to accurately express the true anguish I experienced during those years. At the time, everything felt as though it would be easier if I were dead; at least I wouldn't feel the pain of living anymore. Every special occasion spent with my family was scary to me. Like any child, I looked forward to spending time with them, but my heart would sink when they arrived. My anxiety followed me, even though I hoped it wouldn't. Looking around at the smiling faces of my loved ones, my mind would tell me lies. It would tell me this was the last time I'd see all of them together because something bad would happen soon.

To say my path was torturous wouldn't be accurate. To say it was true anguish wouldn't describe it. The pain was my only reality. I'm sure that today, pain is your reality too.

As I grew older, the doctors told me I would most likely never graduate high school, let alone get a job. Nothing seemed to rescue me from succumbing to the deep, dark prison within my mind.

Despite this, I was determined. I pushed through.

Over the years, I tried every treatment and medication that I could get my hands on. Some things worked for a bit, but nothing provided a lasting cure.

To make matters worse, as time went on, the thoughts I feared most started to manifest. My grandfather passed away. I couldn't deal with the turmoil of my grief. This amazing man, whom I grew up with in the same home, died. My entire life died along with him. He was one of the few people I knew who I could feel safe around. He was sturdy, stable, and kind, but now he was gone. The laughter in my house faded and each Christmas after his death became somber. Those sounds of joy turned into sounds of yelling, crying, and anger. Our light had been put out. My grandfather was gone. None of us knew what to do or how to do it. We went from a loving house of laughter to the most depressing place I had ever been.

My OCD took complete control over my body. Instead of experiencing my grief, my mind forced me to control everything around me. Somehow, my mind told me that it was my fault that he died, and I was forced to take part in every obsession and compulsion imaginable. I even stopped eating.

For the next few years, my life continued to spiral out of control. I experienced trauma after trauma, health crisis after health crisis, funeral after funeral and I was numb.

I was happy to be numb, for if I wasn't, I wouldn't have been able to deal with the stress. I was grateful for numbness, and I still am today. It was in those times of numbness that I learned how to feel again.

"You had the power all along." - Wizard of Oz

The power to heal yourself is something you already possess. The cure is within you.

The reason why we experience so much turmoil is because we have no idea how powerful we actually are. The reason we cannot find this cure is because we feel weak, overdone and discouraged to the point of no return. We have fears that overwhelm us and we constantly worry. Every day is different yet completely the same. Yet, the power to heal is within us. It's right there in your mind.

Anxiety can take so many different forms and can manifest from mild to severely crippling. It can show up as OCD and Bipolar Disorder and can cause severe and debilitating depression. It's post-traumatic, it's panic, and it's numbing.

No matter how it appears and shows up in our lives, it's different, yet all the same.

This book can be applied to the intrusive thoughts, compulsions, and obsessions of OCD; the manic-depressive episodes of bipolar disorder, panic attacks, and post-traumatic stress disorder. It speaks to all anxieties and mental illnesses.

You may be thinking, "How am I ever going to get past this? I'm not strong enough to overcome my anxiety."

I know what it feels like to be hopeless.

I know what it feels like to be weak.

I know that when you've been sick for a long time, you not only feel weak, you are weak.

This is the lie your mind tells you.

Anxiety can make you believe in your weaknesses. It can brainwash you into thinking you aren't as "normal" or as strong as other people, but that's a total lie.

You are not weak at all! In fact, you are insanely strong. You are one of the strongest people on the planet, and I'll explain why.

When you've had to live with a mental or physical illness, and chronic anxiety or depression, you grow massively strong.

You're resilient.

You've battled inside your own head, which is indescribable to anyone who hasn't. Your mind doesn't leave you. You don't get a day off from it. Hell, you don't even get an hour off from it. You can't run away from your mind. You can't go to the gym and leave it behind for an hour. You are dealing with this pain all day every day, which builds a sense of endurance that no athlete could ever touch.

See? Strong!

The things we have had to put up with as anxiety sufferers are totally unbearable and unbelievable, but as hard and as dark as it is, know this - you are strong!

Don't let anyone or any situation tell you otherwise.

You are strong.

When you retrain your brain to know the truth despite the lies it tells you, you will finally be able to live the life you've always believed you could never have. You'll make up for all the lost time because the intense joy you'll feel will be born from appreciating the light after coming out of the darkness. It's about seeing the vast contrast. When you're in the pain, you can appreciate the pleasure that follows more. The pleasure is where we all want to be. So, how do we get there?

This book, like myself, is very unconventional. It doesn't follow any rules and was created to help you navigate your own healing process. People cannot be defined with a one-size fits all approach. Each body and mind is individual and different, so your healing will be too. This book shows you how to permanently heal from your anxiety and actually enjoy the healing process. You see, there are flaws in conventional therapy programs. As much as I believe in facing your fears, you've been challenged enough. Recovery should be easier and more relaxed. Your healing should be a process of natural progression.

Healing of any kind doesn't have to be challenging to the point of crying in a corner.

The shifts in your mindset should be subtle and slight.

I see these common tactics used so often today in the mental health field, which serve to push the mind too hard and too fast into dealing with things it's not ready for.

This method is rarely effective because it just causes more pain and terror. Using the methods that I have created, you will naturally want to face your fears along the way. You won't feel pushed; rather, you will feel pulled into wanting to face your fears. There will even be times you will be excited to do so.

My approach is subtle and gentle.

My method leaves a lasting change.

Take weight loss for example. Do the lasting, lifelong changes to your weight occur in a diet that helps you lose 30 pounds in 30 days? No.

The real change comes from the subtler, less dramatic approaches. Those are the ones that have long lasting results. It's the same with recovery from anxiety and mental illnesses.

I have been practicing the tools in this book for years and years. I have compiled everything that has helped to heal my anxiety and OCD.

Since practicing and applying these tools I have taken back my life. In fact, my life is better now than it has ever been before. I'm actually happy, which is something I never thought I could sustain.

I laugh every single day and I'm filled with appreciation for the things and people I have. I've quit all of my detrimental habits and addictions, repaired and strengthened my most important relationships, and have faced all of the fears that were holding me back. I not only do the things that once terrified me, but I can genuinely enjoy them.

I want these things for you. I believe and know that you can obtain them. You will feel more confident and better equipped to handle stress. You don't have to live the rest of your life in so much pain. In fact, this can be an enjoyable experience. It's time for you to start feeling grateful for your anxiety. Yes, I said it. In the same breath, it is also time for you to tell your anxiety to leave. It no longer serves the purpose in your life that it once did.

Yes, it's true.

Your anxiety, panic or mental illnesses have all served a purpose in your life. You have nothing to lose and so much to gain by reading this book and putting in the work to change your life.

It's time to commit. Take the concepts and tools that I present to you as fact. If you start to question everything, you're wasting too much precious time and energy that you could've spent recovering. With anxiety issues, we tend to question a lot of things and think results are too good to be true. In this case, don't do that. Let the book do its work. I will guide you away from the path of misinformation regarding anxiety and mental illness.

Throughout this book, you will notice some "Journal Breaks."

Take them.

Do the work.

Go out and buy a journal that you love - one you will enjoy using and that makes you happy. Spend extra money on it, so that is a journal that you will WANT to use.

The final step in the book is a transformational 40-day program that I can promise will have long-lasting and life-changing effects on your recovery. I have designed this program to last for 40-days because, in my experience, that is the amount of time it takes to make lasting change.

Commit to this book and to the 40-day program and I know you'll be shocked, yet pleasantly surprised, to see the shifts you'll experience along with the peace and relief you will obtain.

"Your life does not get better by chance, it gets better by change."
Jim Rohn

I can open the door for you, but it's up to you to move through it. It's time to take your power back! I can give you all the information and tools in the world, but success only comes to the people who decide to take their power back and keep moving forward no matter what.

Today, not only have I recovered, but I also live a beautiful life I never thought possible. I truly can't believe how fortunate I am.

I can't believe that after years of terror and intrusive thoughts about speaking in front of my fellow classmates in high school, I can now get up and rap karaoke in front of a bunch of strangers just for fun. I was also able to deliver my speech at my sister's wedding exactly the way I had hoped I would. These successes are not minor for me. I used to be deathly afraid of public speaking because I was always consumed with thoughts of how people were judging me. I can leave my house messy and still feel relaxed in it. I can go on vacation and submerse myself in the experience of just letting go. I feel that childlike excitement in my heart when I talk about my career.

Still, I am not special. I wasn't lucky either. I worked damn hard to get where I am today and by picking up this book, I know you are ready to do whatever it takes to recover. The answers in this book took me a long time to understand when I was figuring it out on my own. That is why I wrote this book for you, so you don't have to waste time as I did for so many years.

Anxiety is not permanent. You may have anxiety or a mental illness, but these are not forever. This is a very controversial truth that I not only believe but have experienced in my own life as well as so many others that I have helped. This is my belief and my understanding. We are here in this moment, but we change and evolve daily. It's true. Anxiety, OCD, depression, PTSD, bipolar disorder, mood disorders, eating disorders or whatever it is that you are suffering so much from, is not forever if you don't want it to be. I've seen many people who suffered from these life-crippling issues find healing.

The fact remains the same — we can heal. You are not sentenced to this suffering for life. If you don't believe me yet, don't worry. You will see the truth.

Chapter 2
Why Our Minds Choose Anxiety

The importance of witnessing and observing our thoughts is undeniably essential when it comes to overcoming anxiety. How often do we just observe our thoughts? I had always been observing my thoughts without even knowing it. I found the human mind fascinating, especially my own. When I was able to identify myself as a person with OCD, I did a lot of research and became incredibly aware of my thoughts and my mind.

"Being the gentle witness of our thoughts" is a concept I first learned from Gabby Bernstein, a woman who was highly influential in my recovery process. She taught me how to become the observer of my thoughts in every area of my life because you can't fix what you don't know is broken. You can't change something that you're unaware of. I can guarantee you that the more you observe your thoughts without judgment, the more everything will begin to become clear to you about your anxiety. When I first started to gently witness my thoughts, I realized how negative and judgmental I was. I was constantly judging others and myself. I would go into the bathroom, look into the mirror and think how terrible I looked and how tired I felt.

I would constantly complain inside my head.

I would worry 24/7.

I was in one place physically and in another mentally. I was worrying about my health, money, and exhaustion while worrying if others would judge me for something I said or did. It was a judgmental parade of thoughts going on all the time.

Although this was very disturbing to me, it was also incredibly exciting and enlightening at the same time. Why? It's because I knew those thoughts could be changed! I realized that all the limitations in my life were coming from inside my own head. They were my own thoughts, and I could change them. Instead of looking in the mirror and thinking I looked tired and drained, I started to think how beautiful I looked.

Instead of obsessing about every word I spoke to others, I started to not care as much because I knew that inside my heart, my intentions were good. I knew that I was doing the best that I could, and if somebody didn't like me, it really didn't matter.

When I started to observe and change my thoughts without judging myself for them, the coolest thing began to happen. My actual life experiences began to change and improve. When I changed my thoughts, I must have been radiating some kind of wild and bright energy because the people around me became kinder and more drawn to me. I felt more love inside that just illuminated from me and onto everybody else. I was laughing more and finding myself in situations that worked out easier. I even started to get more opportunities.

You see, when I changed my thoughts, I wasn't battling inside myself anymore. I had chosen peace. I had chosen my loving, true, and *authentic* thoughts, and the results were miraculous.

This was all a result of a change in my mindset. I've read many books that speak to mindset. They talk about good thoughts versus bad thoughts, positive versus negative, loving versus fearful, and they essentially all mean the same thing - that as a society, we have a tendency to move towards negative thoughts over positive thoughts.

It's way more common and "normal" to complain about waiting in a long line than to say, "This line is amazing! I'm so happy I have this extra time to stand here and appreciate life!"

The point is, we have a natural tendency to complain and think negatively. Talking about how financially broke we are or how much we hate our jobs is considered normal. We have been programmed this way. Society functions this way. We are brainwashed by our surroundings to think, act and feel negative.

As I read books that spoke to mindset, I understood how challenging it is to change your way of thinking. It is not easy for the average person to go against society and change their thoughts. My husband and I would read the exact same books, and I saw how much he struggled daily to implement the mindset strategies. He struggled so much even though he doesn't have the added challenges of OCD and anxiety. This helped me understand how much more of a challenge it is for people with depression, anxiety/circular thinking, and OCD to prevail over the mind. Perhaps the authors of these mindset books couldn't entirely relate to those of us who have had or are experiencing chronic anxiety and mental illness. It's just harder for us.

After reading these books, I felt inspired. I would try out the theories and love the results. However, I began to feel discouraged. I realized that my mind was different. That's when I discovered that I had to write a book that would serve as a guide for people with thoughts and minds like mine. We see the world through our chronic, doubtful, and intrusive thoughts that the authors didn't necessarily consider when writing. We have extra challenges. It doesn't mean that we can't do it, but it does mean that we need an alternate route and different approach.

It may take us a bit more time, and we may need to practice more frequently. But it also means that our results will be better. They will be better because we will learn to appreciate our minds more than the average person. We have been through the darkness to better appreciate the light. It will all be worth it. The light will come. We will excel and, because of the inner strength we have, will actually have an advantage in the end. We will be leaders, an inspiration to others, successful beyond our imaginations, and filled with strength. The greatest victory will come through overcoming something we never thought we could overcome.

Anxious Mind versus Authentic Mind

Let me introduce the concept of the mind. There are two different states in which the mind can be in called the *anxious mind* and the *authentic mind*. You can't be in these two states at the same time. You are either in one or the other. This concept is very black and white. There is no gray area here. You are either thinking thoughts that come from the *anxious mind* or thoughts that come from your *authentic mind*. Throughout this book, you will see me use this concept consistently because it is a vital concept to understand for your recovery, so familiarize yourself with it.

Once you are aware and conscious of the inner dialogue within your mind, you can start to differentiate between the *anxious* and *authentic mind*. The *anxious mind* is a result of your fearful and doubtful thoughts. Our minds also tend to swing towards being *anxious* more naturally. We live in a highly stimulated, competitive and somewhat pessimistic society. People owning their power and potential is not always the norm. In fact, it's more abnormal.

Struggling is considered normal. *We are addicted to struggle*. Even though living within the *anxious mind* doesn't feel good to us, it's still where our thoughts tend to go. We feel like things are normal when we are complaining about traffic, relationships, money or our jobs. Most workplaces in North America tend to be places filled with complaints.

Even though this fact can be eye opening, there is really no one to blame. Pointing fingers at those people or thinking we are better than them is just going to separate us further from our natural state of love and the *authentic mind*. Marianne Williamson speaks a lot on this topic in her book titled, "A Return to Love." She talks about how fear (*anxious mind*) separates us from one another as a society and about how love (*authentic mind*) brings us together.

Fear pops up in unexpected ways. We may not even realize how often our minds delve into fear. Judgment on ourselves and others is fear.

Complaining is fear.

Gossiping is fear.

Pessimism is fear. Even flipping the bird to someone in a traffic jam is fear. These deviations from love are all part of the fearful, *anxious mind.* Anytime you're not in love, you are in fear.

The *authentic mind* is different. The *authentic mind* is exactly how it sounds, our true and *authentic* selves. Just as the *anxious mind* is based on worry and fear, the *authentic mind* is based on love, peace, and joy.

We were born with loving, caring, and compassionate minds. When we were five years old, we didn't worry if we were more fit than our friends. We didn't compare the foods we ate with what others ate. We didn't criticize ourselves for "failing" or judging ourselves on what we said or did that day. When we were children, our minds naturally went to the *authentic mind.* We believed we could do whatever we wanted in life, and no dream was too big for us. If we wanted to be a doctor or become president one day, we just knew in our hearts it was going to happen. Imagine how an adult would react and succeed if he had been raised in a totally controlled, supportive and happy environment that was free from the trauma and the discouragements of others' opinions. I can promise you, anxiety and depression would be close to non-existent if this scenario became a reality. However, that is not our reality. We are faced daily with challenges to stay strong and positive. It's not easy to go against the current. At times, we feel like we are swimming upstream and are trying to gain momentum but remain stuck in the same place.

I felt that way for the first year of my healing from anxiety. I felt that as every day passed, I was taking one step forward and three steps back. It was frustrating, and I felt like no matter what I did, my *anxious mind* continued to take over. I would wake up and say my affirmations, read and get myself in a positive place. I'd meditate and say prayers. I would get myself to a calm place, become grounded and solid before I left for work. Then, I would arrive at work. By lunchtime, I was ready to jump out of the damn window. Complaining and arguing constantly surrounded me. I would go into the bathroom during my break and take some deep breaths to try and refocus myself, but I felt hopeless. I quickly realized the power of my environment. I understood that I could get into a place of the *authentic mind*; however, it was not incredibly easy to sustain it, especially with OCD and anxiety. Everyday, I would revert right back to that place of the *anxious mind* and get lost on the track to success. If it wasn't my work environment, it was drama within my own family. I was getting phone calls from my family, who were always arguing with one another. I was falling into the same old patterns I had experienced before while trying to resolve other people's issues instead of focusing on my own recovery. I would call one person during my lunch, then call the other, run into my house, have lunch, get back in the car and go back to work. I was clearly setting myself up for total failure. By the end of the day, I was fully submerged back in my *anxious mind*. I was complaining and bitter. My anxiety and OCD symptoms were off the charts. I had to decide that this was no longer tolerable to me and make a choice to change.

I ended up quitting my job. Then, I began coaching people who suffered from anxiety, panic, and mental illnesses. This was not an easy choice, but I had to commit to my healing and be unwavering in that commitment. I was willing to do absolutely anything to get rid of my anxiety and OCD. No matter what, we must understand that we always have a choice. We can choose thoughts that will nourish our *authentic* mind or choose thoughts that will nourish the *anxious* mind. No matter what the circumstances are in your life, no matter what tornado of fears are swirling around you, know that changing your mindset is a choice.

No matter how bad your anxiety gets, you always have a choice. Even with chemical imbalances in your brain, you still have a choice. Thinking you don't have a choice is simply a lie your mind tells you.

Recovery is not just about inspiration or motivation either. We are naturally motivated to worry and follow through with addictions, but we aren't as motivated to make the necessary behavioral changes in our lives to bring about the results we so dearly want. This is because behavioral changes are hard. They can be challenging and are definitely not as easy as taking a pill because they take time, patience, consistency and diligence. At the beginning, they can feel like a battle, but in the end, your behaviors will change permanently. Pills aren't helping us. Deep down we know they are not the permanent solution our body and mind so desperately seek.

When I started to realize this more, my recovery began. I made that choice to immerse myself in joy and choose thoughts that would support my *authentic mind*. I did the work, practiced the steps and strategies outlined in this book like it was my full-time job, and I never quit.

At the same time, I changed everything in my life that wasn't supporting me and I promised myself I would get better. This meant throwing on a hoodie and running in the rain when I felt like I had to move, moving houses, quitting my job, and cutting myself off from the people who were causing me chronic stress and anger. My life was a total mess and filled with anxiety triggers. I had to make choices and decisions from a place of peace with my *authentic mind*. This is when I started to notice the transformational changes in my OCD and anxiety. I began to laugh more. I was actually starting to have fun. I gave up my fear of travel and began to see places in the world I had always dreamed of seeing, without being held back by fear and anxiety. I started to feel the moments of fear and obsessive worry dwindle. I started believing in miracles and that I could do more with my life. I pushed aside all of my worries and gave them to a higher power. I knew God had my back.

As I stated before, when these shifts started to happen, circumstances started to change too. My life started to work out for me and the situational craziness and bad luck that always used to occur, suddenly stopped. I even started making more money and began to believe my OCD was not going to control me anymore. I noticed the compulsions and intrusive thoughts I had my entire life were melting away. Whenever they would pop up again, I started casually dismissing and ignoring them. It was a total miracle. The transformation in my life was absolutely mind-boggling. All because I made a choice to feed the *authentic mind* with love, just like I did as a child.

So why would our minds do that to us?

The answer is simple. We have been brainwashed to fear, be skeptical of good, and to worry.

We have been brainwashed by our parents, society and our own negative experiences that we have embraced as beliefs. We have separated from our true states and childlike minds.

As children, we were pure and naturally drawn to love, joy, and excitement. These are the most natural emotions, yet as adults, we shut ourselves out from them. Our lights have been dimmed by the dark realities of the world. We've watched people we love suffer, experienced traumas, and haven't properly dealt with our emotions. These experiences imprint themselves onto our souls and into our minds. This is when our anxiety and depression worsens. We are living in a world in which those who cry are called weak and are told they need to suck it up, move on, wipe their tears and get back to work.

We put labels on things such as win or lose, succeed or fail. Our minds naturally lean towards negative self-talk because that is the natural adult state. We compare ourselves to others and basically measure our success that way too.

Our Childhood and Our Parents Can Influence Our Anxiety

Our parents and families tend to be the most impactful people in our lives. We learn from them and sometimes turn into them. It's no one's fault. Everyone is doing the best they can do with the knowledge they have; however, we need to take a good look at our childhood, upbringing, and family contributions when it comes to our current situation. I want to make this very clear, this is not a place to dump on your parents. This is a place to understand WHY your anxiety is the way it is. It's essential to your recovery to understand where and when you picked up on limiting and *anxious* beliefs. We need to ask ourselves what negative messages our minds received as children and through experiences in life.

For instance, you may not have made the sports team you tried out for at school and as a result of this, you believe that you are a failure at that particular sport. You may have noticed that your father hated his job, so you just assume that it is normal and okay to hate your job. Maybe your mother had anxiety or got really nervous when your grandparents came over to visit; therefore, you get anxious around your parents or grandparents now. These trends can be generational. I've seen anxiety continue throughout generations. This doesn't mean your anxiety is any harder to recover from if you have experienced this. Your family's story doesn't have to be your story. You don't have to share your parent's fate in relation to their career, marriage, or anxiety-wise. The chain is waiting for you to break it. Understand, without judgment, where you may have picked up on some limiting beliefs from your family.

Journal Break

Take a minute to write about some limiting beliefs you have about money, relationships and any anxieties/worries/fears that you feel like you have. Identify where you think they originated from. This is totally judgment free. After you're done with the list, I want you to write, "I love you, I forgive you, and I release you," under each belief. Close your eyes and place your hand on your heart. Picture that person you need to forgive genuinely apologizing to you. This person may even be you. Forgive them and let go of the limiting belief.

If you walk away from this book and know this one statement to be true, I will have done my part in helping you recover.

You have a choice.

You have the power to choose the *authentic mind* over the *anxious mind*. Even though you will experience many situations in which you feel like you are helpless, know that you're not. You can always choose what to think. When I finally regained power over my own life and my circumstances, I chose the *authentic mind* and to heal no matter what. *That* is when I began to heal. Remember, this is not my curse. This is my blessing. It's a part of my story and for that I am thankful.

Chapter 3
The Tripod of Anxiety

"The Tripod of Anxiety" is a simplified formula that I created to explain and break down the three main causes of anxiety.

The Tripod of Anxiety:

Chronic Stress / Trauma + Chemical Changes in the Brain + Your Mindset = Cause of Anxiety

The cause of anxiety can always be traced back to this formula. We may not be able to see all three in our lives, but they are all very present. If you are experiencing anxiety or mental illness, they are there.

The first part of the formula shows that you can either have chronic stress in your daily life or trauma that you haven't dealt with. You can also have both, which honestly, is much more common. Then, we have chemical changes in the brain, which will not be as obvious to us. I will touch on this later in the chapter. Your mindset is the final factor in "The Tripod of Anxiety." Your mindset and outlook on both your anxiety and your life is by far the most important factor in healing. When added together, these are the causes of anxiety and mental illness.

As we all know, no tripod can stand strong with one leg broken. Once one of the legs break, the whole thing comes crashing down. The same can be said for "The Tripod of Anxiety." Our goal here is to break one of those legs within the formula. If one leg is weakened, the tripod falls. All we have to do is weaken just one of those tripod legs to combat our anxiety issues. However, my program works to weaken them all so that you have a much greater chance of recovering.

Now, it's important to understand that none of this is your fault. The tripod develops over time. This is true for all of the tripod legs, including your mindset. You have been lied to by your *anxious mind*, which has convinced you that you have an unwavering and permanent chemical imbalance within your brain. It tells you that you will, inevitably, struggle and suffer. However, your perception truly does equal your reality. When you perceive struggle, your reality becomes struggle. When you perceive healing and ease, guess what happens? Countless studies have been done to prove this. This is not a theory anymore, it is fact. Your perception of any situation equals your experience of that situation. When we can master the change in perception within the brain, the tripod falls apart.

For example, if you perceive a situation to be a boring waste of time, you're going to believe it. If your perception is that everything happens for a reason, this changes your reality. All of a sudden, your world view is completely different and your reality forever changed. Now, I'm going to explain each part of the tripod so that you can fully comprehend this truth and learn how to dismantle it piece by piece.

Chronic Stress/Trauma

The trauma I've endured has shaped me into the person I am today. I wouldn't remove the trauma I've experienced in my life.

It's a bold statement to make since I've been through a lot, but it stands true and I'm grateful for every traumatic experience I've had. However, this hasn't always been my outlook. I still work on releasing the wounds of my past. It's a long process, especially when healing from several traumatic events. I want to share with you some of my experiences to show you that I have been where you are and have revolted against the struggles. Also, I want to illustrate how these events were part of the cause of the development of my OCD, anxiety, and depression.

Now you already know, I was given the diagnosis of OCD at the age of eight. My guess is that I suffered even longer than that since some of my earliest memories of childhood were of me crying hysterically in protest of going to school on the first day, crying every morning before school for a year, and crying even more on days coming back from vacations.

I didn't just cry because I wanted to stay home. I had this deep sadness and depression that was abnormal for a six-year-old. Looking back, it is not surprising that I had this depression since by the time I was six, I had already experienced significant trauma.

As I continued my schooling career, my mom began having severe panic attacks due to her chronic stress and trauma. She started slowly deteriorating both mentally and physically as she experienced these attacks daily. My sister and I tried to help by sitting with her in her times of need and trying the best we could to help. I believe that my passion for helping others began during that period. It was so hard to watch our beautiful and vivacious mother go downhill so fast. That was when I saw the reality of anxiety. It can suck the life right out of you. It broke my heart and still does. Nobody can prepare you for the pain you feel watching a parent, or any loved one, suffer. It's as if you're suffering right along with them.

I lived with my parents, grandparents, and aunt and uncle all under one roof. Since there were eight members of my family, I thought this meant I had to do everything in 8's. If I didn't, I was convinced they would all die by my hand. Chronic stress and trauma had already established itself in my life by the time I was in grade one. One year later, I had experienced sexual trauma at school. I had no idea what was happening was wrong. My OCD then changed from cleanliness obsessions to sexual obsessions. I would have what I called, "dirty thoughts" and would need to confess them to my mother. I was convinced that if I didn't, I would go to hell. I had these thoughts constantly and was literally tormented by them. There was no escaping the thoughts. I had them in bed, in my dreams, at school, and on my birthday. I felt so alone, so abnormal, and so guilty. I switched schools and never told my mom why until years later.

I loved my new school. It was a place where I finally felt safe. After moving there, I had some of the best years of my childhood. I had great friends and together we had so much fun. Of course, I still had the thoughts and they transformed as the years went on. But I was in a much safer and healthier environment.

When I turned fourteen, a close family friend passed away in a freak accident. It was the first death I remember really feeling in my heart. It was so devastating for my sister and I, since we were used to seeing this person around our home. After that, things continued to go downhill.

Before I began high school, the doctors found a tumor in my knee, which led to my first surgery. Starting high school this way was not easy. All of my friends were sectioned off into different groups whilst I was at home recovering. The operation revealed that the tumor was not cancerous, but the doctor ended up botching the surgery resulting in a severe circulation complication. My legs turned almost black from having practically no circulation in them and the doctors told my parents they might have to amputate my leg.

This was such a dark and terrifying time. Due to my hospitalization, I grew sad and lonely as my anxiety and depression took on a new form. As I went in for my second surgery, I began to hate school. I started to experience the familiar sadness I felt when I was six years old except at this point, I was sixteen. I knew it wasn't normal, but I had a deep need to constantly be around my mother. She would drive over to my school at lunch to take me out every day because when I was alone, I thought about committing suicide. I was having severe bouts of manic depression to a point I cannot even describe. I was having torturous thoughts again, but this time it wasn't worry and fear. It was this deep, dark, and crippling sadness. My OCD worsened, too. I would continually obsess about my grades because I felt like they were the only thing in my life that I could control.

When I finally graduated, I was relieved. I graduated with honors and won two awards for the highest grade average in my school and the highest grade average in the district. Undoubtedly, the reason I received those awards was because of my manic obsessions with schoolwork. My OCD was so out of control, it manifested into my grades. This obviously ended up becoming a blessing for me. Sometimes you just have to see the silver lining.

At 17-years-old, my depression began to lift, and I got a job working for the public school system as an educational assistant. The next few years, I immersed myself in my passion for helping children. My OCD and depression improved in huge ways. For once I felt like a normal person. I decided to go to college when I turned nineteen. I was so excited and ready for this next step in my journey. I had great friends and was literally living my life to the fullest for the first time ever.

Little did I know, the summer months to come would be the most traumatic of my life.

One afternoon, whilst out at a restaurant, my drink was spiked with a pill that caused my body to react badly. Things deteriorated rapidly, and I was rushed to the hospital. I almost died, since the dose I received was more than my system could handle. I had one collapsed lung and the other on its way.

If my friends hadn't rushed me to the hospital in time, who knows what would have happened? That's grace right there. I've had many moments of grace in my life. Even though I physically recovered from that traumatic experience, an even bigger blow was coming my way that would have me emotionally recovering for years to come. My grandfather, who I loved more than anything, got very sick and passed away quickly and without warning. I speak about him many times throughout this book because he was such a rock for me. His death impacted me more than I could've ever imagined. Instead of grieving, I hid my feelings away and my OCD manifested into a severe eating disorder. The eating disorder went on for years and years and eventually caused many chronic health issues.

Throughout the next ten years, one of my friends died from meningitis, my other friend died after being hit by a drunk driver, many family members got sick, many other close people to me passed away, and I suffered from serious health issues. I was brought back to the hospital after a concussion I received, as well as an electrolyte depletion disorder that I developed from the physical trauma my body endured.

I literally could go on and on here. I feel like my life has been trauma, after trauma, and the truth is, it has. The point of this is to show you that no matter what situation you are in right now, you can get better, too. The non-stop trauma I experienced in my life caused my mental illness and anxiety to worsen.

I became numb. The more trauma I experienced, the less I dealt with my feelings. I couldn't shut out the worrying thoughts I was experiencing and began to have emotional breakdowns and panic attacks. I was in and out of the hospital, experiencing terrifying physical symptoms, as well as getting diagnosed with life-threatening illnesses.

I was a mess, and I didn't see a light. I was worn out and exhausted. I was totally discouraged. I felt like I tried everything, yet nothing was working. I was getting worse. I will share with you my breakthrough later in the book, but to say I was living in pure hell wouldn't even begin to describe it accurately. The bottom line is, the trauma made my anxiety so much worse.

However, as horrible and traumatic as those events were, and as much as they helped to cause further anxiety, OCD and depression, if I hadn't gone through them, my life wouldn't be in the position that it is today. I would have no idea how to write a book like this. I would have no idea what to say or how to help anyone going through anxiety, other than what I learned about in college. I would have no life experiences of my own to help others rise up from the pits of the hell that is anxiety. I would be just like any other coach/therapist who has never truly experienced what it actually feels like to go through anxiety or mental illness, yet is very quick to give you advice on what you're doing wrong. I actually have a huge advantage in my field because of all this. That's why I feel the need to help so many people. I know where they have been because I have been there and recovered from it.

It's also important to understand that trauma does not always look like trauma. Sometimes trauma can be something from our childhood that we now view as insignificant, but the effects of this event have been imprinted in our subconscious mind. Perhaps you were bullied as a child and now you struggle with low self-worth. Perhaps your mother screamed at you for eating too many sweets and now every time you eat a cookie, you feel guilty. Be aware of these events. As subtle as they may seem, they have been imprinted into your memories and into your soul. Do not discredit their detrimental power.

Chronic stress is another very important factor to remember when it comes to anxiety. It can make your life feel like total chaos. Maybe you're a single parent who is constantly being run into the ground, or maybe you work at a very stressful and draining job every single day. Maybe your home life is difficult and there is constant arguing. These are all examples of situations that contribute to chronic stress. The way to heal is by making changes that focus on tangible solutions. Perhaps you need to consider a new career or hire somebody to help around the house. Maybe you need to move, or perhaps you need to distance yourself from the individuals who are causing you anger.

When I say change, it has to be a pretty big change, especially when you are recovering. If your goal is to immerse yourself in joy, then chronically stressful situations are the enemy of that goal. However, I'm not saying you need to make these huge changes all at once. In fact, doing so is not the best for people suffering from anxiety. I'm all about taking baby steps because I've seen the impact of them. Slow and steady wins the race here. The first step is to simply become aware of the necessary changes.

Journal Break

Take a look at your life. Are you chronically stressed? Pull out your journal and list some of the things causing you stress. List 2 possible solutions for each. Some solutions may seem unrealistic or impossible, but write them down either way. It's good to become open and aware of these solutions, even if you're not ready for them or are unsure if they are the right solution. Don't stress about this, as you don't need to make these changes now; it's simply an exercise of awareness.

Chronic stress can also be a result of unhealed trauma. You will find that unhealed trauma can seep into areas of your life that you never even thought were connected. For example, if you lose a close friend or a coworker, as I have, you could experience chronic stress every time you visit a certain place because you are reminded of that person. When I speak about chronic stress, I am talking about situational things as well. Perhaps you have a chronically stressful job, or maybe the job itself is traumatic. I used to work with children who had been through severe abuse and some of them acted out in very violent ways on a daily basis. My job was chronically stressful during those times. Chronic stress and trauma can actually intertwine within one another.

Chemical Changes in the Brain

The most common theory in the medical field today is that mood, behavior, and anxiety disorders are caused by imbalances of neurotransmitters in the brain. These neurotransmitters are serotonin, dopamine, and norepinephrine. However, what doctors don't tell you is that these neurotransmitters can be balanced naturally. There have been many studies done on the causes of mental illness but not many done on the permanence of them. No study has proven, with certainty, that these imbalances are permanent. Yes, we may be experiencing anxiety and mental illness NOW, but that's not to say this is a life sentence. The chemical imbalance analogy is accurate, but what isn't accurate is the impression it leaves on the sufferer. So, if you are currently experiencing a chemical imbalance, then yes, you are going to have extra challenges in your mind and body. However, with the ability to change your outlook and mindset, along with reducing chronic stress and dealing with your trauma, you can correct these chemical imbalances.

Another powerful imbalance that affects mental illness and anxiety is cortisol. Cortisol is a hormone and can also have a huge impact on the imbalance of neurotransmitters within the brain. Cortisol is made in the adrenal glands and helps the body manage stress. When we are in an emergency situation, our body goes into fight or flight. This is when cortisol spikes. This is a totally natural reaction to a situation that needs our attention fast. Anxiety, however, comes into play when cortisol spikes up and the body is not necessarily in an emergency or survival situation. Anxiety and mental illness sufferers almost always have issues with their cortisol production. I have had both chronically high and chronically low cortisol. Chronically low cortisol occurs when the body has had enough of being in fight or flight all the time. When you have consistently high cortisol for years, which most anxiety sufferers have, the body gets exhausted. It can no longer keep up and that's when low cortisol, also known as adrenal fatigue, occurs. In this stage you become very tired and must slow down in order to repair those adrenal glands. Things like mental illnesses, depression, and anxiety will pop up and be an issue for you with chronic cortisol issues. It's important to understand that almost every human being has some imbalance within the body, which in turn causes imbalances within the brain. Some imbalances within the body cause problems within the brain such as anxiety, depression and mental illnesses. Other imbalances cause the body to have digestive issues or diabetes. It's all individualized because every body and mind are different.

When your body starts to calm down consistently (through many tools I provide in the book), the cortisol production in the body will then begin to normalize. When this happens, the imbalances of neurotransmitters within the brain will begin to balance as well, but the key here is consistency: you will not heal overnight.

You didn't get to where you are overnight, so as such, the healing process takes time. Patience and consistency are key. The more we consistently weaken this leg of the tripod by practicing relaxation, correcting vitamin and mineral imbalances, changing mindset and reducing stress, the more easily we can correct the brain. The chemical imbalances will balance; just give it time and stay dedicated.

A common misconception out there in the medical field is that only prescription drugs can help these imbalances. This is completely false, and we all know it. We know deep down that the mental health system is broken. We know that these drugs are not healing mental illnesses. In fact, in the long term, I see more often than not, people feeling worse, not better on these drugs.

Another misconception is that these imbalances are a lifelong struggle. I can't tell you how many times a doctor or psychiatrist told me this, and the same thing has been told to so many others.

The chemicals within our brains are way too complex to explain here, but the causes of the imbalance are even more complex. Yes, we may be experiencing imbalances, but the reasons for them are so incredibly complex because there are SO many things that can affect the balances within the body and brain. Doctors and scientists have made many advances because of research, but they haven't even come close to understanding the complexity of the body and how everything affects the other. If one of your bodily systems is "off" or not optimally working, the entire system can be impacted. Doctors will quickly write a prescription for issues with our brain system without completely understanding the process and side effects of the pill they just put in your hand.

Doctors are not to blame. They are only passing on the information they learned in school. What they don't tell you is all the different possibilities and reasons for your ailment. They don't tell you because they are unaware. Medical school is a school, and like any other profession, they can't teach you everything or you would never graduate.

We need doctors because they save lives. I'm in no way insulting doctors or those in the medical profession, but I also have to stand true to the goal of this book, which is to inform and help in every way possible.

This information is so vital for you to understand so that you can take your healing into your own hands and become an advocate for your health. It's important to be aware of how the health system works before you blindly begin taking pills that may not actually benefit you long term.

In a doctor's office, the assessment process is quick. You usually describe your symptoms and are prescribed a pill. You don't often have a doctor that asks you in depth questions and tries to find the root causes of your illness. Instead, you take your prescription paper and go about your day. You fill the prescription, take the pill, and possibly see the results in a couple of days. You may even feel more relaxed, calm, and clear at first. The question I always like to ask is how are the pills making you feel after a few years? These pills can work at first but rarely are long-term solutions (as I'm sure many of you have experienced). You're not getting the results you want simply by taking pills. This is because chemical imbalances in the brain can mean many things that the doctors aren't telling you. These things can be anything from vitamin and mineral imbalances to hormonal imbalances.

If you're currently on medications for depression or anxiety, I'm not telling you to get off of them. In fact, stay on them during the course of this book and for as long as you feel you need them. I'm a true believer that you will know the right time. You are your best doctor. Quiet your own mind so that you can hear the answers for yourself.

Once you manage to get you more in tune with your mind, thoughts, and body, you will know the correct time to wean off your medication if that is your choice. If not, that's completely fine too. I don't know your individual case, but remember, your doctors often don't really know your body that well either, only you do.

That's one of the biggest messages I want you to take away from this book: you are the boss. You are in control and totally capable of taking on that role. You are smart enough to know what pills to take, what to do, and what to avoid. No two people are the same, you must become comfortable with tuning into your mind and body. The same things will never work for two different people. Trust me, I've lived this. I can't tell you how many doctors were shocked by some of my health issues. Many times, they were confused when I had a weird reaction to some pill they gave me. There were times I didn't feel comfortable taking a certain medication, but I ignored my intuition and felt much worse afterwards. This goes for both doctors and naturopaths.

I've heard many times, "Wow, I've never had a patient have that issue in all the 30 years I've been in practice."

I would just politely smile, knowing that no two bodies are the same. What works for some people will not work for others. That is a fact. This is why our medical system is so badly broken. One pill will not react the same in two different people, even when it appears to have the same effect. As a teenager, I took one pill for over 13 years for a hormonal issue and it caused a severe electrolyte imbalance. Other people had nausea or stomach issues from taking the same pill. No two bodies have the same reaction.

The good news is that we can improve our imbalances substantially by dealing with our trauma, reducing chronic stress and making some changes to our daily lifestyle. Our mindset can also reverse imbalances within the body, and I'm going to explain how.

Outlook and Mindset

"The most important decision we make is whether we believe we live in a friendly or a hostile universe." -Albert Einstein

Changing the mindset can actually have a powerful impact on our bodily chemical imbalances. When adopting a mindset of, "I will never get better," or "I have a chemical imbalance that will never change," you will not have a chance of long term healing. That is why these particular sufferers never actually get better.

Have you ever noticed that people who constantly tell themselves and others that they will never get better actually never do? Mindset holds the key to recovery. It's the focus of this book. I have never seen one patient heal without first working on their mindset.

Mindset is the number one tool for reducing cortisol levels in the body. Remember, your perception of reality becomes your reality. Mindset calms down all of the systems in the body, which allows them to function better. Utilizing the power of mindset also improves the chemical imbalances within your brain. This can take time. As I said earlier, your body feels as though it has been under attack for years with your anxiety; it needs time to heal. You need to be consistent with your mindset changes, and it will take some time for your chemical imbalances to catch up with your improved mindset. This is why it's so important to be patient and consistent.

Let's take a minute to explore mindset. What do our eyes see? How do we process the experiences that happen to us? As humans, we are constantly taking in information. We are experiencing, seeing, and interpreting things in our own ways. Each person has a different chemical balance within their brains that is totally unique to them. There is absolutely no such thing as a normal brain. We are all normal and abnormal in our own fascinating and unique ways. We all think and process the world differently through our mindset. We must ask ourselves these questions: What lens are we using? Is it a lens filtered through the eyes of resentment, pain, and fear? Or is it a lens filtered through the eyes of love and patience?

One person may view life as challenging, unrewarding and discouraging. Another may view the world as miraculous, beautiful, and full of opportunity. These are two very different views and provide two very different experiences. How do you think life will turn out for the person I described first? How do you think the second person I described will experience life? Do you think success in career and relationships will differ? What about happiness and even health? Of course, they will be vastly different.

The same goes for anxiety. Some people view mental illness or anxiety issues as a death sentence. This is totally understandable. No one can possibly understand the torment sufferers experience unless they have lived inside our heads and have seen the world the way we have. Our brains are structured differently, and we process the world differently than others. It's not a problem. It's just that we see things differently, but so did some of the most famous artists, actors, and billionaires. So really, we are in good company.

Over time, our *authentic* mindset weakens while we constantly deal with anxiety. You may not even notice it, but if you're still having anxiety issues, there is undoubtedly work that needs to be done in this area. It is imperative to our recovery that we work on our mindset and our outlook. I have seen time and again the great successes of my clients that have focused particularly on the mindset area of recovery. This makes total sense too, since anxiety and mental illness form within the mind and thoughts.

We can start by changing our language and self-talk to fully support the mindset.

Instead of saying, "I'm damaged, I'm broken, I have trust issues," say: "I'm healing, I'm rediscovering myself, I'm starting over." - Horacio Jones

After taking my first set of antidepressants, and having them fail miserably, I remember thinking, "I have this chemical imbalance that I can't control and can't help, and now even the drugs that are supposed to help me correct that imbalance aren't working? What am I supposed to do now? Where am I supposed to go from here?"

Automatically, I would revert to the *anxious mind*. My doctors would also keep telling me that I would always struggle to get better and that I was sick and broken. How could that not be exactly what I believed and felt, especially if my trusted doctors were telling me so? I struggled chronically, and I didn't know of a time when I hadn't. However, we need to rise and stop identifying with words like "broken" and "sick" because we are neither.

We will use the concept of the tripod throughout this entire book. The rest of the chapters are purposefully designed to weaken the legs of the "Tripod of Anxiety" so that you can heal permanently. Like I said at the beginning of this chapter, no tripod can stand without 3 legs. We will weaken them all, one by one. This book is broken down into sections that will help you weaken the tripod. Section one focuses on "breaking the leg" of chronic stress and trauma. Section two "breaks the leg" of chemical imbalances and section three "breaks the leg" of negative outlooks while strengthening the *authentic mind*.

Chapter 4
Anxiety's Unique Potential for Joy

As you know, anxiety is terrifying. Mental issues are horribly dark. Absolutely no one can understand it properly unless they've been through it. No one knows the constant fear and worry that goes on in your brain. You can't take a day off from your brain or a vacation away from your mind. You can't stop constant thoughts. You go in the shower, they are there. You're eating dinner and you're worried. You're trying desperately to fall asleep but you're just too anxious to do so. So your mind starts racing and you can't stop. You feel alone. You feel darkness. You can't move. You can't take deep breaths, and you can't think of anything but your fears. Your throat closes, the muscles in your face are tight. You're often silently thinking, worrying, and fearing.

When others advise you to just "do something different," or tell you that you "aren't trying hard enough," you really just want to smack them. It's true; people just don't get it. People that haven't been through it have no idea how crippling it is. It's exhausting and takes a toll on every part, angle and corner of your life.

I'll be honest, I have some unconventional and potentially unpopular opinions in this book. This book was created for the "outside-of-the-box" thinker. This is not for people who just want to survive their anxiety problems but for those that want to thrive. My goal for you is that you will have the ability to experience genuine joy and childlike excitement that you may have lost. One of the unpopular opinions I have is I believe we actually hold an advantage when it comes to experiencing joy. Yes, you read that correctly. I believe that anxiety and mental illness sufferers have an advantage over the average person when it comes to feeling intense joy and happiness. Allow me to explain.

During my years of helping children, teenagers, and adults move past their mental health challenges, I've noticed this one, revolutionary observation. The people who are determined and recover, appear to have a higher threshold for joy than the average person. Yes, it's true. As odd as it may sound, when these people recover, they experience greater joy than the average person. There are two reasons for this. One reason is that they've experienced such darkness and hardships, they appreciate the little wins they start to have during recovery. When you take someone who has been through hell, and you show them a little bit of heaven, they tear up and can't believe their eyes. They are overjoyed by what they see and experience. They see the flowers, they smell the smells, and they are enlightened. In reality, this could be something as small as being able to sit in a restaurant for an hour with friends. Anyone else would look at this as a normal night out. Tiny victories become huge victories when it comes to anxiety. We have the gift of genuine joy for the little things because we can't always do the little things. I remember a time when I felt so incredibly happy just because I packed less for a trip, a place where OCD had always run the show. I was actually overjoyed by this accomplishment. Something the average person would never think twice about, was an opportunity for me to feel indescribable happiness.

Intense joy is not common these days. This is because adults don't know that kind of joy is still readily available to them. They believe that this kind of happiness is reserved only for children. Funny enough, kids know that intense joy and happiness is available to us all. As adults, we are brainwashed and conditioned to stop believing in that kind of joy. Just like we stop believing in things like magic and the tooth fairy, we grow up and adjust our beliefs to those which are acceptable by society. That is why, when we were children, we were closer to our *authentic minds*. We believed.

The other reason we have a higher potential for joy is we often feel our emotions to the extremes; therefore, we have equal potential for intense darkness as we do for intense joy. Stay with me here for a minute. We are all familiar with the challenges one has with bipolar disorder in which emotions can come in waves and extremes. As much as a bipolar person can experience extreme pain, they also have the immense capacity to experience extreme joy. This is not just a symptom of bipolar disorder either. All people with mental illness and anxiety experience these extreme emotions. It's in our make-up, and it's our special gift. Yes, to the sufferer, it seems like those extreme emotions always lean towards intense sadness and despair, but we can channel that energy into extreme joy. We can re-direct that energy from negative to positive. We have something here that others don't have: we can experience the beauty that they can't. Our potential can be misused and misdirected. I view this potential for joy as God's little gift to us since we've been through so much darkness. It's a way to balance our lives, if you will. With extreme pain comes extreme joy.

I remember a time when I was recovering from a lot of my obsessions and compulsions, and my husband and I were driving down this beautiful road on a late summer's night. We had the music blaring, the windows down, and I could smell the beautiful scents of the flowers and feel the thickness of the water heavy in the air around us. I was able to close my eyes, listen to the music, and actually feel the air on my face. I was filled with this incredible, extreme sense of gratitude, joy, and freedom. I smiled to myself and realized I was crying. My husband asked me what was wrong, as I tend to not be someone who cries too often. As I looked up into the sky, as cliché as it may sound, I took a deep breath in and told him I was finally free. I smiled and felt so much joy in my heart that I thought it was going to burst. He could see it in my eyes too. He turned to me and said, "Wow, you can experience such intense happiness. I wish I could feel that."

Now, this is not to say that my husband can't experience it too, but my point is that our potential to experience joy comes more naturally to those who have been through our pain. That moment was one of the many moments in my recovery where I experienced that intense joy. There really is nothing like it.

I know so many people that have this unique ability to see the world differently. This book is going to help you tap into that side of yourself so you can receive this gift of joy. I'm here to teach and guide you through a different way of thinking. I am going to completely reconfigure the way you look at your anxiety.

Our success and recovery starts to seep slowly into our lives. This is the exciting part: when we practice holding onto that joy and those *authentic* thoughts, we shorten the gaps between our times of joy and despair. This is what Gabby Bernstein talks about: "the gaps." Her theory is that when we are recovering from addictions, anxiety or depression, we can simply measure our successes by how long these gaps are. The chunks of time of joy start to get longer in between those chunks of time we spend in *anxious mind*. The more we practice the theories and practical tools I provide for you in this book, the shorter the fearful time chunks get and the longer we can extend those joyful periods. As soon as you know it, the joy will start to become easier than the fear. It takes time, patience, one-step-forward-two-steps-back types of days, but it happens, and when it does, the joy is incredible. It's not just about vast comparison of extreme darkness to extreme joy, but we can experience extreme emotions more easily than non-sufferers because we can use those tendencies to our advantage. We can direct our focus, drive, and brainpower right towards *authentic mind*.

Anxiety Is Your Advantage in Life

Some of the most brilliant minds out there suffered from mental illness and anxiety. Some could even argue it helped them become who they were meant to be. The world may not have some of the most spectacular artwork, movies or advances in technology if it weren't for those brilliant minds. Isaac Newton was said to have depression and suffer from bipolar disorder, Michelangelo and Leonardo Dicaprio were diagnosed with OCD, and Abraham

Lincoln had regular anxiety attacks and suffered from depression. Anxiety has no bias. You can be making a million dollars a year or be homeless. Anxiety has no reservations for whom it touches but one thing we all have in common is superhuman strength.

This strength is our gift. It's as though God himself knew we could withstand such pain and yet come out stronger than ever before. Think about it logically; who can withstand what we've gone through and not be incredibly strong? The worst part is that instead of feeling that superhuman strength, our *anxious minds* actually trick us into thinking we are weaker than most. So here we are, with our superhuman strength, walking around feeling as though we are actually weaker than a "normal" person. The strength we have other people don't understand and frankly can't even comprehend. There will be a point in your healing when you will actually be grateful for your anxiety. I know that may be hard to imagine now, but it's coming.

We have our own unique gifts and I have actually discovered in my findings and experience, that different anxiety sufferers have varying gifts and strengths. For example, people with OCD are determined as hell. If you've ever met anyone with OCD, they can probably put up with more than you can ever imagine. Research has actually shown that people with OCD have a much higher level of determination than most people and are two times more compelled to learn new things. We tend to have excellent memories and are incredibly empathetic towards other sufferers and people in the world. Anxiety sufferers are said to understand things on a deeper level and have stronger levels of intuition. People with depression tend to be smarter than the average person and have a better perspective of the world. We suffer, but we are creative and great at observing. We tend to be more introspective and outside-of-the-box thinkers. The beautiful side to having anxiety is that it can be viewed as our special gift. There are so many similar characteristics in people that I have both worked with and have known, that I can honestly say these statements are so incredibly accurate.

We all view ourselves as having certain advantages and disadvantages. Some of us feel as though we were dealt better or worse hands than others. Anxiety and depression can be categorized as one of those things. When people suffer from these invisible disorders, it's very easy to look at them as having a disadvantage. You may even envy other people who seem to do things with such ease; things that you can't do, or things that terrify you. We are changing your perspective on that. Whatever your "disadvantage" may be, attempt to look at it as one of your gifts. Think of ways in which your disadvantages have become advantages in your life. Perhaps you have learned a lot from the challenges you've had to endure or you've been able to help others. You may even have a new perspective and appreciate things more. When we start viewing life in gratitude, that's when amazing things begin to happen. Anxiety is just another step in our lives; a step we must take to move onto much greater things.

Imagine if you were told as a young child that if you had an anxiety disorder you were gifted, blessed and even had special gifts and talents because of it. What would that do to change your perspective on anxiety, depression, and OCD? I always wondered who first decided that anxiety and mental illnesses were disadvantages. It's odd because everyone just followed suit without question. Everything in life is a thought and a concept, which needs to begin and end somewhere. The concept of anxiety being a disadvantage ends here.

We can actually be the generation to change the way people view anxiety and mental health. Anxiety is our asset; it is actually an advantage to us in our careers and lives. We have better memories, better gut instincts and are more creative and compassionate. These four traits alone mean that we should be able to put an anxiety disorder on our resumes. Seems far-fetched, doesn't it? Well, it doesn't have to be.

We can be a part of a movement that pushes society in this direction, but I need more people on board with this theory and way of thinking so we can all be alive in a time where massive change happens. A time when people are no longer ashamed of their anxiety, depression or mental illnesses, but are instead proud of them. In a way, it is your job to overcome your anxiety and mental illness in order to show others that it can be done too. We can't teach others how to help themselves if we haven't been along the path. Take note of your journey and the important things you learn along the way, so that one day you can share the things that I may have missed. Anxiety is your gift, so use it.

We must feed ourselves with the knowledge that we can be healed and we're not broken, but instead, we're just different and have beautiful attributes that other people don't have.

Chapter 5
What Holds Back Success?

First of all, I want to make something very clear, you can't fail. Failure doesn't exist. It's true. Think about it: failure is simply something we feel when we are disappointed in ourselves. So, in actuality, only we can create failure.

Consider this: who decides what failure is? What is failure to you? When do you consider yourself to have failed? Think about these questions, because it's not something that we evaluate too often, but we must.

There were many roadblocks that came up for me during my healing, and this is very natural. It's all about how you deal with them. I would have weeks when I would wonder, "What's the point?" I had a concussion, fights with my family, work drama and illnesses. It was a very difficult time for me and I felt, on numerous occasions, as if I were failing. It wasn't until I understood that only I could tell myself I was failing, that I really learned the lie that failure is. Failure is *anxious mind's* best bud: they work synergistically together to create great pain in our lives. Whatever your perception of failure is becomes your reality. If you thought failure meant getting a "C" on a test in school, you would've likely felt as if you failed when you received that particular grade. Some students looked at a "C" as great success. Someone learning a new skill would surely celebrate a "C." It's all about the perception of failure. That's the only thing that makes failure real. You either win or you learn from situations in life. You can never really fail.

Fear of Being Free from Anxiety

Fear is at the core of all our anxiety. Deep down, we even fear our healing from anxiety because we are used to having it. The thought of it going away is so foreign to us that we actually fear it. I remember how I used to get so frustrated with people who didn't seem as though they wanted to heal. I felt like I had the answers they needed to get help but everything I said to them, they would resist. Over time, I realized they were afraid of healing. Anxiety is a disease of fear and doubt, so of course anxiety sufferers would fear and doubt their very healing. Having this fear is a real thing for many people. Usually, you don't even know you have this fear, but it's there on a subconscious level. It's not that we don't want to heal from our anxiety, because we very much do: it's that deep down we have a fear of what healing may look like.

We are so accustomed to living and dealing with anxiety that we don't know what will happen to our lives if it's gone. We don't like uncertainty and fear getting better because of it. As much as we want to move past this stage, anxiety is safe. We are used to it, and can somewhat predict it because we know it so well. Our *anxious minds* lie to us and tell us that our anxiety is a certain and stable thing in our lives. I felt comfortable with the early onset of my OCD, even though it was total torment because I didn't know anything else. In a backwards way, the thought of it going away was actually kind of scary because it was so foreign to me. I had lived my whole life with OCD and didn't know what life would be like without it. We tend to avoid the things in which we are not familiar and comfortable with. Change can be unsafe to us and safety is very important to anxiety sufferers.

Sometimes, on a subconscious level, we even feel like we receive secondary benefits from sickness. We may receive extra support from loved ones that we otherwise may not have received. Or perhaps we are people-pleasers to the core, and the anxiety is a reason to opt out of the things we don't want to say no to. For instance, when I was at the peak of my anxiety, I actually liked the extra support I was getting from people. Don't get me wrong, I was in misery, but my husband was there for me. I went through so many traumas, and it was a way for me to retract a bit and finally have someone take care of me and make me feel safe. I felt like I deserved some empathy.

In the back of my head, I worried what would happen if I got better. Would I still get the support and love I so desperately needed? However, when I started to heal, the coolest thing happened; I actually felt more love and support. I started feeling better and gave myself the love and kindness I always longed for. I never lost my husband's love and support either. When my mood started changing from anxiety to my true loving self, I started making choices with my *authentic mind*, and he caught up with me. He, too, started making choices through his *authentic mind*. I became a leader for him to cope with his own experiences. When two people are in a relationship and they both start making choices out of love, the relationship gets so much better. I feel safer and more loved now in my marriage than I ever did.

I know this topic is a sensitive one for most. Believe me when I say that it was a sensitive one for me too. When I first heard that I could be keeping myself from recovery on a subconscious level, I was pissed. How dare someone suggest that I was doing this to get extra support from people! How dare they claim I'm keeping myself here for secondary benefits! The more I worked through my stuff and did the personal work, the more I understood and realized that I indeed was keeping myself stuck in anxiety. This is definitely not true for all cases. You may have worked through all of this and not have these issues at all, but for the ones who can relate, there is no shame in feeling this way. This is to simply give you that moment of clarity you need in order to get better. Remember, all of these things are happening on such an intense subconscious level that you are, for the majority of the time, totally unaware of them. No one is to blame here, especially not you.

One realization that set me free was that sickness does not equal love. Somewhere down the road, we were inadvertently taught that sickness equals safety. I know I was. On a subconscious level, I was taught that to be sick meant that I was safe, and it somehow equaled love. These are lessons taught to us on a level we aren't even aware of, and we absorb this information by people who are totally unaware of it themselves. The limiting belief that sickness equals love and safety is very common amongst families who are hard workers: people who burn the candle at both ends. When they feel they can't take anymore, their bodies and minds collapse. Sickness = safety. This can be the body's way of protecting itself. Sickness is also a good reason to care for yourself.

If you don't practice daily self-care, your bodies and minds crave it and you breakdown. When you breakdown, you can then start to rest, take it easy and care for yourself properly.

I watched my mother suffer for years. I was young when her panic attacks began, which internalized a message to me that said, "This is normal. This is safe." As a child you don't question things like this, you just accept them as normal. You figure every single family and mother go through this terror. When you are children you just accept these circumstances as facts and they become your beliefs about the world. I then believed that anxiety and panic equaled safety. We must teach ourselves that it is safe for us to heal and that only good things will come from healing anxiety. We will not lose anybody's love or care if we heal.

Another common block that stops us from our healing is the fact that anxiety has become part of our identity. We begin to wonder what life will look like without our anxieties, depression, and panic because they are such a big part of who we are. Who will we be without them? *The anxious mind* tries to convince us that we have no idea who we really are or what we will really be like without anxiety. This is false. We have equal opportunities at all times to return to our *authentic minds*. Don't fall for the *anxious mind's* vicious lies.

The *anxious mind* tries so hard to take the magic out of our lives. It tries so hard to convince us that we are being unrealistic when we want to heal and believe that we CAN heal. Being pessimistic and skeptical comes so easily when we are thinking from a place of *anxious mind,* but why is that the way it has to be? We question the beautiful miracles too often yet accept pessimism so easily. When bad things happen to us, we don't question them at all. We just accept them as fact. We are so eager to destroy anything we can't explain like the magic and all the healings. Even the things we can explain, we are more motivated to discredit if they are positive things then if they are negative things. That's just the way the *anxious mind* works, especially in this modern society. We have spent so much time strengthening that *anxious mind*, no wonder the *authentic mind* is so far out of reach for us. We really need to start rethinking the way our society and minds work. Perhaps *anxious mind* is the only reason for all the bad things in this world. I'm so sick and tired of watching people get bogged down by life. I'm exhausted by watching this all unfold in front of me. It's so defeating and discouraging to see people that just don't experience the happiness that they can have. This is all *anxious minds'* fault. Remember, we can always choose to return back to the *authentic mind*.

The minute you decide you want to recover, is the very moment in which you begin your recovery. The *anxious mind* wants a quick fix, but we want something that lasts - and quick fixes don't. As an anxiety sufferer, you have a choice and that's hard to believe. When we feel like we've tried so incredibly hard but nothing works, we obviously come to the conclusion that we have no choice in the matter. We believe we are a slave to this master and cannot escape, and "screw you" if you think my suffering is a choice! This is not the full picture, my friends. **This is not a life sentence. This is**

not your destiny. In fact, down the road, anxiety is going to be something you are eternally grateful for.

Listening to Everyone's Advice!

Another reason we struggle in our lives and our recoveries is that we fall into the trap of doing what other people think we should be doing. We have all asked for opinions and needed that validation before. The problem is when we constantly act and make choices based on what other people think we should do, we lose ourselves. We stop trusting our gut instincts and stop following our hearts. We can feel trapped in a life that we don't want and can become resentful. Let's avoid all that and learn to trust ourselves. If you feel like you want to do something "out of the norm," then learn how to trust yourself. That's how amazing and unique things happen and change occurs.

The lasting change is not going to happen by you just doing what you think you should do. Really, my best advice here is to stop listening to advice! Start listening to your gut and yourself. I remember when I finally came to this realization. I had been going to all these doctors, trying all these treatments, and spending all this money. I was still getting nowhere. I knew deep down that I needed to deal with underlying trauma from my past and lower my levels of chronic stress. I knew I had to rest and take care of myself and my healing would come. I even instinctively knew that I had a vitamin deficiency in my body, even though no doctor was catching it. I read articles on magnesium deficiency and instinctively knew that I had one. I could feel it when I finally slowed down and listened. This is the key here – listen to what your body and mind are trying to tell you.

Journal Break

Put your hand on your heart. Close your eyes and ask your body what it needs from you. What is the first thing that comes to mind? What actions do you have to take to give your body what it wants? This is important and you have to understand this - you are your own doctor, guide, and therapist.

One of the hardest things anxiety sufferers experience is feeling alone. We feel so alone in our heads all the time, so sometimes we over-ask peoples' opinions - and trust me, people LOVE to give you their opinions. You can't blame anyone for this either because they are just trying to help. What you must understand is that you are your best yardstick. Some of the free online support groups are great, but don't overuse them. We can easily fall into the trap of information overload and becoming totally overwhelmed and confused; therefore, reinforcing the limiting belief that life is discouraging, hard, and we will never get better. With too much information and opinions rushing toward you, it becomes increasingly difficult to quiet your thoughts and actually listen to what your *authentic mind* is saying. You may be wasting a lot of your listening time on others and not on yourself.

Hitting Bottom

Hitting bottom is a good thing. Some of my most "bottomed out" times that I threw my hands in the air and felt like giving up, were the most powerful moments. I may have given up for a day or two and just cried it out, but I needed to. I would look at those days as an emotional purge, ridding myself of negative emotions that I had to release. I looked at those days like a shedding of the skin. Sometimes giving up is the best thing for you. It's true that you can only go up from here. When everything hits the fan, it usually means that you're going to break down. Breaking down is good for people with anxiety. It helps you rise up like a phoenix from the ashes.

The only way to ensure that change will happen is through your commitment. It is the only 100% guarantee that you will achieve change in your life. If you want to change, commit to change. I love the famous quote, "Nothing changes if nothing changes." If you are living the same life day in and day out, don't expect anything in your life to change just because you think or hope it will. Switch things up! Life was not meant for us to be walking on a hamster wheel. We decide if we make the same mistakes over and over again. When you're feeling trapped in your recovery and are having some "stuck days," know that it's a good thing. It just means that you are weakening your *anxious mind* and it's trying to fight its way back in. Don't fear this. It's a sign that you're getting better.

Situations We Are In

Life's situations can contribute to your anxiety. We have many things that can set us up for either success or failure. Maybe your job is stressful or you really don't find much enjoyment from it. Maybe you live in an abusive situation at home. Perhaps you're dealing with a sick parent. Or maybe you just simply feel unfulfilled or without purpose in your life. No matter what situation you are in, you can make changes that will support you in moving forward. Even if you are in a challenging daily situation such as caregiving for a loved one; there are still things you can put in place to make life easier and supportive of your own recovery from anxiety. I actually see a lot of caregivers with anxiety and depression issues. See, we are very compassionate people as a whole. We know what it's like to suffer, so when we see others suffer, we want to help. That is beautiful, and it's our gift but sometimes it can be too much for us as well. We need to be very careful and always look and evaluate our life's situations.

We all have these little things we need to patch up, so consider taking steps to patch up these strains on you. Create a supportive life around you. Take a step back and look at the big picture. You can do all of the work and employ all the strategies, but if you are distracted by the situational hang-ups that are adding to your anxiety; you will take longer to get better. Your focus will be on those situations and not on your healing. We will talk more about this in the book, but remember you can always choose to make decisions with your *authentic mind*. Stop telling yourself that it's okay to do stuff that you hate and causes stress such as staying in a job you hate, spending time with people who treat you poorly, and running yourself into the ground day in and day out.

We have to remember that peace does not come from situational stuff. Peace comes from within you. That way, no matter what happens in the world around us, we have the ability to close our eyes, put our hands on our hearts and return back to our inner peace and calm. No matter what tornado of drama is swirling around you, you can make a choice to stand strong in your true peaceful state. It does help, however, to eliminate that tornado of drama. We were not created anxious - we became anxious. In the same way, we can become peaceful by choosing our *authentic mind*.

Trying to Get Others to Understand

It's incredibly useful to try and build support around you, so you can get your loved ones to understand what you're going through. However, don't wait for them to give you permission to recover. If you wait for support to get through this, it may never come in the way you want it to. Be your own support system. We also talk about spirituality in this book, which has been my number one support throughout my recovery. Don't get me wrong; it's great to have support from other people. It's great to have someone to talk things out with and share your struggles and triumphs. Sometimes, though, people aren't supportive. They have their own stuff going on. As anxiety sufferers, we aren't the only people in the world who have fears and limiting beliefs. We need to know this truth and understand it. Be kind, forgiving and patient with the people around you. Change your expectations of them and create change in your life that totally supports you. Don't wait for others to get on board, or you may be waiting forever.

Impatience

Every simple shift towards the *authentic mind* is healing. There are countless treatments that fail due to impatience. Now, I'm not suggesting that you stick with something for three years after seeing no results at all. I'm talking about the times when you give up after three months and dismiss a treatment plan as being ineffective because it didn't give you the results you wanted in your desired timeframe. This is when we have to release control and let go of our expectations. I have an entire day dedicated to this concept in the 40-day program at the end of this book. Learning how to release expectations is an integral part of your recovery, as it allows your healing to happen naturally.

The true key to success is to believe in the outcome before it happens: to be certain and sure that everything will work out before the results even occur. This is a huge reason why so many people "fail" at things. It's not failure, but impatience camouflaged as failure. We put in a few months, maybe even years, of work into something that we truly want, but we don't realize that stuff takes time. It's the people who stick it out that succeed.

The best thing you can do is to start accepting yourself and your anxiety for where it is now and to be happy with that. Be grateful for your life in this very moment. This is challenging, but practicing it allows it to become more natural to you. Just because you accept where you are right now, doesn't mean you are going to stay there. In fact, the opposite is true. When you calm down about what is going on in your life, become patient with where you are right now, big change will happen naturally and more quickly.

Chapter 6

The Secret to Success is Consistency and Positive Routines

Practice makes perfect. Unfortunately, these kinds of phrases tend to lose their significance and meaning as we age. We start to dismiss them as being too simplistic. The truth is that these things were taught, emphasized and repeated to us as children for a reason. In relationships, practice makes perfect. In baseball, practice makes perfect. In mastering a new job or skill, practice makes perfect. You get the picture. This is also true for recovery from addictions, mental illnesses and anxiety disorders.

We tend to talk ourselves out of things and overlook the simplicity of some solutions. For instance, I recently started juicing fruits and vegetables. Within no time at all, I started feeling much better and my body started healing. Yet, for so many years I kept looking at juicing as such a simplistic solution to my health that it couldn't possibly do that much for me. Instead, I would look for answers in pills and supplements, thinking I would need something "much stronger" than just simply juicing. When solutions seem too simplistic, we figure they can't have as much of an impact on us as a pharmaceutical pill or quick fix. This practice of avoidance is exactly what keeps us sick. We talk ourselves out of stuff all the time; therefore, we never fully commit to healing. If we believed in our healing with every bit of energy and effort, we would be better before we know it.

Your commitment to your recovery must be unwavering. This means that you must be dedicated and keep promises to yourself, despite the challenges that come. If your car breaks down, you argue with a friend, or get fired from your job, your commitment must stand strong. Your recovery is the most important thing in your life right now. Failure to make recovery number one is no doubt the top reason why people don't get better. You must commit fully and know that it takes time and consistent dedication to heal. If you want it bad enough, you'll successfully recover.

Journal Break

A letter of commitment

I have found this exercise to be transformational. In your journal, write out a letter of commitment to yourself. You will begin the letter by telling yourself how excited and proud you are of the new life you are embarking on. You are going to thank your anxiety for all the lessons it has taught you. Here you can list some of those lessons as well, but then release the anxiety and tell it you no longer need it. You will now state your promises and commitments to yourself. P.S. If this feels strange at all to you, it's supposed to. It's a good sign.

An example of a letter to myself is this:

Dear Tosha,

I am so proud of you for making the choice to commit to your recovery from OCD and anxiety. I am excited for the life you are about to embark on. I am going to honor your dreams and desires and promise that I will be patient with you. I love and accept you as well as forgive you for anything you have done in the past that has contributed to the anxiety. I respect you enough to now make a choice to choose authentic thoughts over anxious thoughts. I will now identify my anxious thoughts and call them out as being lies. No matter what challenges arise in my day, I will put the time aside to fulfill my commitment to recovery. I understand this will not always be easy, but I know if I stay committed, I will succeed. I want to thank my anxiety and OCD for making me strong and compassionate. I appreciate that they served me at some points in my life, but I am a new person now. I no longer need to be sick. Sickness does not equal safety to me anymore.

Love,

Tosha

When you have completed the letter, post it somewhere or save it in your phone. Look at this letter daily and anytime you need a reminder. This will help you re-commit and remind yourself that you are ready to do whatever it takes to get better.

The next thing I want you to do is practice something positive daily. I have laid out so many tools for you in this book. Use them. They weaken every leg of "The Tripod of Anxiety," thus ensuring your inevitable success. It has taken you years to be brainwashed into the way you think now, so you must counteract that with daily exercises daily. You will be happy made the commitment to heal. We have been brainwashed to choose fear over love, anger over forgiveness and blame over understanding. It's the way the *anxious mind* keeps us stuck. The good news is that you can retrain your brain.

Choose several exercises and incorporate them into your days. This can be a gratitude list, journaling, prayer, affirmations, meditation or visualizations. Start dreaming and believing that life can be better than you ever thought possible. The 40-day program at the end of this book was designed to reinforce this concept into your life for 40 days. It's an incredibly powerful program. Just remember that it's the successful people that have mastered diligence and patience. They work hard, even when the outcome is not in view.

Fight Repetition with Repetition, Fire with Fire

Repetition is the key to solving anxiety. Set yourself up for success here and not for failure. Know in your heart that this is one of the most crucial things you need to take away from this book. Our minds thrive on repetition. Just observe how many times *anxious* thoughts repeat. You need routines in place for success, and you also need to be incredibly repetitive, especially in the beginning. In the beginning of recovery, people can easily start to try something new and get discouraged very quickly after a week or two if they're not seeing the results they hoped for. Let me assure you that nothing in here is a quick fix. All of these things take time and consistency.

We have to submerge ourselves into our treatment. We have to be repetitive to the point of extremes because that is what we're dealing with in our own heads anyway. We have to fight fire with fire and one extreme with another extreme. When we have incredibly intrusive, negative thoughts, we have to fight that fire with incredibly positive and joyful thoughts from the *authentic mind*. This is actually easier than you think. Isn't that a relief? I know you've been dedicated in the past. I'm saying you need a different kind of dedication now. You need time to heal and go through the process with a soft but steady dedication that overrides any discouragement, refocuses you when you're down, and helps get you moving towards your goal of recovery. You want to recover, so therefore you will.

Chapter 7
Five Senses of Peace

How many times have you been in a place of fear and worry and just couldn't pull yourself out of it no matter what you did? During circular thinking episodes, a panic attack or anxiety, we can experience some intense physical symptoms. I used to always feel extremely disoriented during my worst times of stress. I used to feel as though I was walking around in a dream, totally detached from reality. I couldn't think clearly and would wonder what the reason was behind this intense fogginess. It took me a while to actually make the connection between my disorientation and anxiety. Deep down I knew they were probably connected somehow, but I didn't realize HOW connected they actually were. I would walk around and people would be passing me on the street or talking to me and my vision would be distorted as if I were in a movie. It was a very scary experience.

I frequently experienced these episodes during vacations. I know now that the reasoning behind this was my own resistance to relaxation. I believed and submitted to the lies my *anxious* thoughts told me. They told me I was unworthy of a vacation, that I didn't know how to relax, and that my OCD and chemical imbalances totally prohibited me from relaxing. The more I worked the tools in this book, the more I realized what a lie it all was. At the time, it seemed so real, and I believed the lies. What I didn't realize was that I was strengthening my *anxious mind* without even being aware of it. I was telling my *anxious mind* that it was right, I would always inevitably suffer. I realized I needed an effective tool to help me on these vacations. A tool that quickly returned me back to my *authentic mind* and weakened the tripod.

As I've said before, the goal is to weaken each leg of "The Tripod of Anxiety," which is:

Chronic Stress/Trauma + Chemical Changes within the Brain + Your Mindset = Cause of Anxiety (The Tripod)

After a lot of trial and error, I finally came up with my favorite tool for returning back to the *authentic mind* and that is, "The Five Senses of Peace." I created this tool to work synergistically to dismantle every leg of the tripod. It is by far the best tool for overcoming anxiety. "The Five Senses of Peace" is a set of five steps that work harmoniously to quickly calm, ground and redirect both the body and mind. The purpose of this tool is to use it throughout the day. At the beginning of my recovery, I used this tool probably six times a day. When I had to use it that frequently, that's exactly what I did. I did whatever it took to heal. That's what you have to do as well. You can't overuse, "The Five Senses of Peace.' It does not lose its power. It may feel repetitive at times, but in that repetition is where you find your healing. When I began to weaken my tripod, vacations started to become more enjoyable. I surrendered to my panic and accepted it. I adopted an, "it is what it is" attitude. This attitude was helpful because it instantly took away the pressure I had put on myself to enjoy these vacations. When you release expectations and accept what is happening to you, you will quickly return back to your *authentic mind*. So, when do you use "The Five Senses of Peace?" The answer is anytime you experience anxiety, panic, or are feeling stuck in worry or circular thinking.

"The Five Senses of Peace" provides simple steps that you can use during a panic attack. These steps were designed to bring you back to a place of calm. When the body is in a place of calm and the breath is slow, the mind eventually follows automatically. Sometimes when you are in the midst of a circular thinking episode or a place of pure fear and worry, it's very hard to just simply choose better thoughts. We need a "911" kind of helpful tool. This is it. "The Five Senses of Peace' refers to the five traditionally recognized methods of perception and sense - your five senses. You will start with your first sense, which is *listen* and then move on to the second sense and so on. Let's break each sense down.

The Five Senses of Peace

LISTEN to the lies the anxious mind tells you.

SPEAK the truth of the authentic mind.

BREATHE in the calmness of the alternate nostril breath.

SEE that you are safe.

FEEL the environment around you in curiosity and wonder.

First Sense: **LISTEN**

The purpose of this sense is to listen and hear what the *anxious mind* is telling you. You are acknowledging the lies, limiting beliefs, fears and worries that are consuming you. These lies can feel so real. In fact, most of the time, they don't feel like lies at all. They feel completely true and realistic. During this stage of listening, you will pull out your journal and record all the lies, worries and fears the *anxious mind* is feeding you. For example, you may be worried about an upcoming meeting at work and the *anxious mind* may be telling you that:

"You're not ready for that meeting. You're going to sound so stupid. What if you get dizzy again? What if your partner doesn't do their share of the work?"

These are the thoughts you will write down in your journal. It's almost as if you are in one of those retro cartoon shows where the main character has a mini devil on one shoulder and a mini angel on the other. The *listen* sense would be recording the words of that mini devil. The voice putting you down and making you feel like a failure, which are all examples of the *anxious mind*.

As an alternative, if you find yourself in a situation in which you can't journal, one alternative would be to type it into your phone or go for a bathroom break and complete the five senses in there. If you are unable to do this, you can say these *anxious* thoughts aloud or just focus your mind on them. These are suggestions for the times in which you can't write in your journal. I want you to be prepared for any situation, and the journal is ideal for this sense.

(This exercise helps to weaken the "mindset" leg of the anxiety tripod.)

Second Sense: **SPEAK**

You will make counteracting statements to the ones you made in the first sense of "listen." All those limiting beliefs and lies that your *anxious mind* was feeding you during the first sense are about to be dismantled. This is where you tune into the thoughts of the *authentic mind*. This is time for the cute little angel to speak. You are going to now speak the truth. These are the loving statements. You will speak to those worries and fears. We are here to set them straight. In your journal, you will write statements that oppose everything you just wrote down during the "listen" stage. This will counteract your concerns. You are to respond as if the *authentic mind* is speaking and comforting you. This will sound like: "You are healing" *not* "I am healing." These messages are coming from a dialogue within yourself. Don't worry, the more you practice this, the easier and more natural it will come. You're tuning into a caring, kind, and understanding part within you.

I will use the examples from above to respond:

Anxious Mind Lie: "You're not ready for that meeting."

Authentic Mind Truth: "You're going to kick that meeting's ass tomorrow!"

Anxious Mind Lie: "You're going to sound so stupid."

Authentic Mind Truth: "You are beyond prepared for this. You will be able to share your gifts with others tomorrow. Get excited for that!"

Anxious Mind Lie: "What if you get dizzy again?"

Authentic Mind Truth: "If you get dizzy again, you know the proper tools that will help you. The power lies within you. If it happens, it happens for a reason. You have more important things to do in this life. No need to worry."

You are now going to say aloud, with your hand to heart, all of those *authentic* responses. You are not saying the lies of the *anxious mind* aloud EVER or acknowledging them as truth, since they are lies. You are ONLY saying the *authentic mind* responses aloud. Make sure you say these with conviction. Be convincing and say it with feeling. You can rub your chest or your leg in a kind and safe comforting touch as if the most comforting person is right there with you.

Alternative: Again, if you find yourself in a situation in which you can't journal, some alternatives are to type it into your phone, going for a bathroom break and completing "the five senses" in there or focusing your mind on them. Again, the journal is ideal.

(This exercise helps to weaken the "mindset" leg of the anxiety tripod.)

Third Sense: **BREATHE**

During this stage, you will practice alternate nostril breathing. This is a popular yoga breath also called *Nadi Shodhana.* This is my favorite breathing technique for quickly calming down the mind and body. I can't explain how many times this breath has gotten me out of a difficult situation with my OCD and anxiety. It's literally been a lifesaver. Alternate nostril breath has been proven to reduce anxiety and balance the brain by breathing oxygen into the right and left hemispheres of the brain. This is the best breath for instant calm. This breath is known in yoga for helping to dramatically reduce stress and balance the nervous system. You can practice this breath anywhere. I've done it on an airplane, in the subway, at work, anywhere. I love it because I feel like I can do it subtly, without anyone noticing. You can sit or stand while practicing this breath. Your spine should be straight if you can. The left hand can rest on your leg or by your side throughout the entire practice.

1. Take your right thumb and press down on your right nostril, breathing in through your left nostril for a count of 5-10 seconds.

2. Still using the right hand, swiftly cover your left nostril with your index finger, while simultaneously removing the thumb from covering your right nostril.

3. Breathe out through your right nostril for a count of 5-10, the slower and longer, the better.

4. Hold your hand and fingers in that position while you inhale through your right nostril for a count of 5-10.

5. Still using the right hand, swiftly cover your right nostril with your thumb, while simultaneously removing the index finger from covering your left nostril. Breathe out through your left nostril for a count of 5-10.

Repeat. Do at least 10 sets of these. The goal is to bring your body down to a place of calm. Remember that after every exhale, you hold and keep your fingers in the same position as you inhale once, before changing the positioning of your fingers. You want to be breathing in through different nostrils each time.

Alternative: If you're in a public place and feel too uncomfortable to practice this breath, just breathe in through your nose for a count of 5-10, hold it for another 5-10 seconds, and breathe out for 5-10. Again, this is just an alternative. Alternate nostril breath is still the most effective breath during this stage.

(This exercise helps to weaken the "chemical imbalances" leg of the anxiety tripod.)

Fourth Sense: **See**

During this stage, we are seeing that we are safe. We "see" through visualization during this stage. We have calmed the body and the mind and now we must visualize that we are safe now. We must understand that we are new people now. We are not our parents, our families or our partners. We are also not our old selves. We no longer have to be those people. We are not our anxiety or our mental illnesses. We are safe and secure.

Take a minute and place both hands on your chest in front of your heart. Close your eyes and take a deep breath. Visualize the safest person you know. If you don't have or never have had that person in your life, try to imagine God or even someone from a book or a movie; a character in which you associate love and safety with. Decide on this "safe person" beforehand. I want this safety person always in your mind to use for both this SEE sense as well as the SPEAK sense, as they will be your comforting voice of the *authentic mind.* Make sure to write a description of this person down in your journal at some point. I want you to really know who they are. You now continue deep breathing and repeat the following mantra either aloud, whispering, or in your mind.

"You are safe now. You are loved. You are strong."

Visualize your safe person saying this to you as they hug you and hold you in their arms. They are reassuring you that you are safe now. You have nothing to fear and you are in a place of peace. They are also reminding you of your incredible strength.

This exercise helps bring you to a place of safety. Feeling safe can be challenging beyond belief for people with anxiety and mental illnesses. The reality is that you are OK and safe. The *anxious mind* tells us lies that we aren't, but the *authentic* and loving mind shines the truth upon us.

(This exercise helps to weaken the "trauma and chronic stress" leg of the tripod, since feeling unsafe is a feeling most associated with trauma as well as chronic stress.)

Fifth Sense: **Feel**

I love this final step because you can continue this step for hours if you'd like to. This final stage is a grounding technique that brings you back to a place of calm, curiosity, and your *authentic* youthful state. Remember as a child how you would notice and become curious about the environment around you? Do you remember asking your parents a million questions? Do you ever notice how many questions children ask? As adults, these constant questions can be annoying, but it is just plain curiosity, which is an *authentic* place within their souls.

In this stage, we slow you down and bring you back to this childlike sense of curiosity. We open up your eyes to really notice your surroundings, ask questions, and come back to a place of wonder. You almost want to imagine your body moving in slow motion. Remain calm and let your fingers linger on objects around you. Visualize yourself slowing down to a snail's pace or as if your body were walking through water. With childlike wonder, you will walk around marveling and in awe of everything around you while you touch things and observe their tiny details. You slow down, smell things, and allow all your senses to become wild and alive. You become grateful for things you normally take for granted. You marvel at the world around you with an open mouth, in awe of what you see. You smile to yourself, enjoying your new found sense of calm.

You can practice this last sense anywhere. Perhaps you're in an office building. You may walk over to your desk and touch the table or the wall. You may admire the wood your desk is made of and notice the pictures on the wall. Think to yourself how cool it is that this building was built by people and once was nothing. This is a grounding practice.

As you may have noticed, people with mental illnesses and anxiety often have heightened senses. We can be extra sensitive to perfumes and smells, or even tags on the backs of our shirts rubbing on our skin. When you suffer from anxiety and mental illness, these simple everyday things can cause more despair and irritation than they do to the average person. What we are actually doing in this stage is using that sensitivity to our advantage. We are using it for good instead of bad. We are tuning into that heightened sensitivity and enjoying it. I love trying to go outside to experience this sense as I touch flowers, softly smile to myself, and take some time to get curious and sit in awe of life.

Alternative: There is none. You can practice this anywhere and under every circumstance.

(This exercise helps to weaken both the "mindset" and "chronic stress" legs of the anxiety tripod.)

There are some ways in which to enhance the five senses experience for yourself after you have completed the steps. I highly advise people to stay away from technology for at least a half hour after you complete "The Five Senses of Peace." Technology has been proven to increase anxiety, and I've found the five senses practice most effective if you give your mind and body a break. I also suggest for that same half-hour that you don't ask for other people's advice. Often with anxiety and panic, we feel so desperate that we reach out to other people for help.

Don't let the five senses steps overwhelm you. Practice them, and they will become your best friend in recovery.

So, to use as a quick reference, put this into your phone storage or write it on a piece of paper and carry it in your wallet. Use and repeat these five senses throughout your day. Repeat it like it's your full-time job. *The more repetition, the weaker the tripod becomes.*

Five Senses of Peace

LISTEN - Record the thoughts of *anxious mind*.

SPEAK - Respond to the thoughts of the *anxious mind* using the truth of the *authentic mind*.

BREATHE - Alternate nostril breathing.

SEE - That you are safe.

FEEL - Your authentic, childlike state of curiosity and wonder.

Section One
"Break a Leg": Chronic Stress and Trauma

As I spoke about earlier, each section in this book is created to weaken each leg of "The Tripod of Anxiety." One by one, we will help dismantle each leg. The following section focuses on dismantling chronic stress, as well as trauma.

Chapter 8
Honoring Feelings and Emotions

We start to weaken the trauma portion of the tripod by learning how to honor our feelings. As I was sitting here writing this book, my radio started to play the song "What a Wonderful World," by Louie Armstrong. I instantly knew this was a little nod from my late grandfather. This was the song he asked me to put on the CD player in his hospital room a few days before he died. I remember sitting there in the hospital and watching him silently mouth the words to this song. I memorized every detail of that moment. I can remember where I was sitting, what I could see, and what the view was like outside the window looking out onto the hospital's parking lot. Every single time I hear that song, it takes me right back to that moment and the image inside my mind. In the past, I would always have a tendency to turn the song off and move on with my day. Today, however, I noticed that I couldn't continue to write. The song hit me hard, so I allowed myself to be hit hard. I sat down on the floor, put my back against the wall, held my knees up to my chest, and cried while the song played. When I say cried, I mean cried quite hysterically.

In this moment, I was honoring my feelings.

So often, we equate being numb to being strong. We try not to cry during the times we want to cry and for that reason, we consider ourselves to be tough and strong. This is so common amongst the anxiety and depression community. We stuff down our feelings and refuse to honor how we feel. We don't grieve, cry, or get angry when we feel these feelings because we don't want others to judge us. We don't want to look weak by exposing ourselves. However, those feelings don't just go away when we don't feel them. They actually stay settled within our bodies. They become an anxious energy and the more times we stuff our feelings down, the more likely we are to have both anxiety and depression. I make it a point to set aside times to cry when I want to cry. I don't allow myself to just turn the songs off anymore. In fact, I turn them up and play them on repeat until I have cried so much that I can't cry anymore. With crying especially, it's very hard to re-enact, so when an opportunity presents itself, I do it. It's hard to trigger tears later on. So when it comes to crying, I don't put it off. If I have to excuse myself and go into a bathroom, I do it. Crying is a great way to let out your emotions. Don't let those emotions get stuck inside of you. They will come out eventually and the more you stuff it down, the more likely they will come out in the form of anxiety, panic and depression.

One of my many beautiful life teachers taught me the importance of this. She once told me that even when she's in a supermarket and she stubs her toe, she yells out loud from the pain. She doesn't hold it in or breathe through it, as to not make a scene. She doesn't concern herself about the sound she makes, or how she looks to others. She just makes the loud noise because she would rather have an embarrassing moment than have that anxious energy floating around in her body. It's so very unhealthy to suck in your emotions, so let them out. Honor yourself and your feelings. You are a human. You have depression and anxiety, but those are not the only words that define you. You are a person, with feelings that are meant to be felt. We must stop suppressing our feelings. Suppression of emotion does not equal strength - there is no suppression badge to be earned. "Sucking it up" has its place on the football field, but not in other areas of life. Feel the feelings, they need to be released.

Now, some of you may be feeling confused by this:

"OK, so how do I feel my feelings? Don't we always feel our feelings?"

Well, no, not really. We are an incredibly numb society. We don't tend to share our emotions too easily, and this goes for both men and women. As women, we are in an age where we desire to be strong, independent, and seen as equals to men in the workplace and in all areas of life. That's great. I'm all about feminism and consider myself a solid one at that. However, and I'm paraphrasing here, I once heard Marianne Williamson talk about how in this age of feminism, women are abandoning their emotions and femininity. It blew my mind when I heard this, but it just made so much sense. We function in such a highly masculine world that men and women are having trouble embracing their emotions and knowing the difference between masculine and feminine. We are "go go go" all the time with a "suck it up" mentality and a "work till you drop" attitude, which is great for productivity, success and getting stuff done. However, for people predisposed to anxiety and depression, this is not a good mentality to have. We need to relax, rest, and make time to honor our minds, emotions and bodies. It is not weak to feel. I don't care who you are. It's something that needs to happen or you will inevitably become an anxious robot.

There are so many ways that we avoid feeling our feelings and more often than not, we use other things to replace our feelings. Addictions are a perfect example of this. Eating disorders and drug and alcohol addictions are one of the most common ways in which people try to numb themselves and avoid feeling and honoring their feelings.

Journaling can be a great tool to use for feeling your feelings. Writing them out or writing a fake letter to someone who has hurt you can be very therapeutic. Sometimes you may need to do some kickboxing to release your anger. Whatever the emotion is, find a way to feel it and release it. You don't want that bad energy just circulating around inside your body. It's a recipe for more anxiety.

Trauma Work

The main reason why people have issues feeling their feelings is because they are numb. Numbness is often a result of trauma that has not yet been dealt with. Dealing with trauma can be difficult. Often people want to avoid dealing with their traumatic pasts; however, this avoidance simply doesn't work. When the body and mind initially experience trauma, there is often a shock to the system. Trauma rarely comes into our lives in a subtle way. It comes in with a bang. When that happens, our system always goes into some form of shock. We all have different ways in which we deal with the shock. Some of us hysterically cry, which is a good release, but some of us deal in other ways. We many go outside and light up a cigarette, stop eating, binge eat, or get drunk in the midst of trauma. The problem is, when we use things outside of ourselves to deal with trauma, the trauma doesn't just disappear because we want it to. It tends to stay within us and often manifests itself in unhealthy ways within our minds and bodies. That is why I always advise dealing with past traumas. Deep hurts from your past take time and patience to heal. You may need to deal with the same trauma over and over again before you feel peace. Don't feel intimidated by this. Do it at your own pace and never rush trauma healing. Some of the most successful trauma work takes time and is done in very small baby steps. So how do we actually deal with trauma? The answer is everyone deals with it in different ways. I will talk about some of my favorites, but I encourage you to explore the ways that best fit you.

There are many different options online for dealing with trauma. I personally had to try a few different things before I found what really worked for me. Talk therapy with a therapist who specializes in trauma work can be great. It's important to find a person who you really like and enjoy their presence. So often I see people go to therapy because it's what they think they should be doing, but it just isn't working for them. You must find a person who you like to talk to and who gets you. I have talked to many therapists over the years and only two of them were people I actually enjoyed speaking with. They also happened to be the most effective people for me.

Eye movement desensitization and reprocessing (EMDR) has also had a lot of success in helping people deal with trauma. During an EMDR session you follow a sequence of steps and often visually track a moving light or object. You will focus on the traumatic event or negative thoughts during this session. Sounds can also be used in EMDR. I always find these new therapies really cool and always suggest you try them before you dismiss them as being too outside-of-the-box for you. Some of the most effective tools in my life have come from things I wrote off as being too strange for me at the start. Hypnotherapy can also help for trauma victims and can be a transformational experience. Group therapy is another option and is a great way to connect with people who have been through similar circumstances. Like I said, there are so many options out there. Look some things up and promise to maintain an open mind. Some things will work for you and some you may feel don't, but trust me, even the things that you feel don't help you always teach you something new about yourself and your healing. Nothing you do is a waste of time.

Tapping

I first discovered tapping through my personal coach. She introduced me to this concept of EFT (Emotional Freedom Technique). It's a procedure used to overcome many emotions that haven't been released yet that may fester in your body. You can use it for trauma, grief and even daily emotions such as anger and frustration. There are unlimited amounts of these step by step videos online. My personal favorite, Brad Yates, has the best tapping videos on the Internet to date, in my opinion. You may want to come home and turn on a tapping video if you find yourself in a situation in which you feel intense emotions but can't release them. I always suggest to my clients to tap daily at the beginning of recovery. You tap on different meridians on the body while saying positive affirmations out loud. Videos make it very simple to follow; however, once you become a pro, you can do it by yourself and make up your own affirmations. This is an incredibly powerful practice, one that will no doubt cause you to release some stuff that is dormant on the inside of you. When people talk about avoidance of feelings, tapping is a great solution for that. If you shove your feelings down, try tapping. It's empowering, calming and an all-around effective technique.

Transition Out Of Emotions

As much as it's important to feel and honor your feelings, it's also equally important to do something for yourself to transition out of these emotional states once you've finished releasing emotions. Some self-care practices come in handy here and we will talk more about self-care in the book. One way to transition could be to take a bath or meditate to calm the mind and body. You can always work through "The Five Senses of Peace" after you have released your emotions. Do something fun here, too. Sometimes I like to blast music and dance really crazy after releasing emotions. Doing something fun afterwards helps to ground you and enables you to return to a positive state and your *authentic mind*.

The Need to Feel Safe and Heard

All human beings have a need to feel both safe and heard. This may feel like an impossible task because sometimes we have unsupportive people around us. The beautiful thing about this is we can actually do these things for ourselves. We don't need a supportive partner, parent, or best friend for this. We can make ourselves feel safe and heard.

Journaling is a very powerful tool. By writing down and working through your emotions, you can really come to terms with the things that make you feel unsafe. You can then take action in order to change them.

Another option is to pay someone to fill this void for you. It may not sound too appealing, but trust me, it works wonders. This is where therapists and coaches really can help. I always say to people that if you don't have that person in your life to help you stay on track, hold you accountable, and make you feel safe and heard, then pay someone to do it. It really speeds up your recovery process. So, consider that. Also, know that you can have both a coach and a therapist at the same time. A coach can't replace a therapist and vice versa. They are both incredibly helpful in accelerating the speed of your healing process and are irreplaceable resources. With that said, there are several other ways in which you can make yourself feel safe and heard.

Some of mine are:

- Feeling my emotions, instead of ignoring them

- Talking to people who make me feel safe and unconditionally loved

- Cuddling with a soft blanket and pillow (as silly as this may sound, this helps us to soothe ourselves, which in turn helps us to feel safe)

- Prayer

- Meditation

- Placing the hand on the heart when you get anxious (you can subtly do this anywhere)

- Tapping

- Massage

- Heat and warmth of any kind (heating pad, sauna, cup of tea, warm bath or shower)

- Visiting your "happy places"

- Watching your favorite movies, reading your favorite books

- Listening or reading personal development books/audios/videos online

Another way to make yourself feel safe is to give yourself an "out" in situations that make you feel unsafe. Perhaps you want to try and go to a social gathering but feel nervous about it. Give yourself a backup plan or a way in which you can leave if you feel too stressed. I used to do this all the time. Often if you give yourself an "out," you won't actually take it, but just knowing it's there may help you feel safe enough to face something in your life. For example, I used to tell myself that it was OK to only stay out for an hour. I used to tell myself that if I wanted to leave a place, I could. I gave myself that permission. I even took it so far as to give myself an "out" when I was trying to quit smoking. I took it one day at a time and told myself that I could always smoke a cigarette if I wanted to. I actually never took that "out," but knowing it was there helped me decide to quit with ease. Just remember, if you take the "out" it's still a win. It's still a win because you're trying and being consistent. A time will come when you won't take the "out." Again, this will be a natural progression and a comfortable process. Don't force or rush it.

Explore the things in life that make you feel safe and take note of them in your journal. Also, be very aware of the detrimental things in your life that make you feel safe but are no longer serving your highest good. For me, it was a long time before I realized that sickness equaled safety for me. When I was sick, I gave myself a break and allowed my body and mind relaxation and the ability to recoup. Addictions also kept me feeling safe. I used cigarettes to numb myself and feel like I had power. They gave me confidence. It was something I hated myself for. It's good to become aware of all the things, good or bad, that make you feel safe.

Journal Break

What keeps you feeling safe? What habits or routines would you like to eventually eliminate that you feel keep you stuck? What positive habits, routines, people or things make you feel safe that you could add into your days?

Chances are if you're reading this book, you don't feel 100% safe. That's OK. You will. Do the work and then repeat it, and it will slip in when you least expect it. You will start to notice that you are okay and safe.

Chapter 9
Self-Care

Self-care is something you can't overlook. It is so necessary, not just for anxiety sufferers, but for everyone. Truly taking care of your body and mind will ensure you will have success in your recovery. Self-care is taking care of yourself, just as you would a child. Some of us feel as though we were not taken care of as children, as much as we would've liked to have been. This can be a reason as to why we struggle in this area as adults. Today is our opportunity to make up for it and this is exactly how you must view self-care. It's an opportunity for you to make up for whatever you've lacked. It's not depriving or denying yourself of your desires anymore. It's giving into the things that make you feel loved and comforted. Only you can do this for yourself. Only you can choose *authentic mind,* which adores self-care. I really want to emphasize the importance of this. You cannot overlook it because you will not get the success you want if you do.

Self-care is not just for you, either. You owe it to the world to take care of yourself. The world needs the love you have to give as well as the gifts you have to offer. There are so many people out there who are suffering, especially people with anxiety and mental illness. It's our job to love and help others. If you don't take amazing care of your body and mind, then the world misses out. You think you're helping your family or your job by pushing your body to do those long hours while not resting or vacationing enough, but you're not. You're actually doing the opposite. When you burn out, you're literally no use to anyone. We've heard this before in the preflight instructions on an airplane. The flight attendant always instructs you to, "put on your oxygen mask first, before you put on your loved ones beside you."

You won't save a life if you can't breathe.

Self-care is taking care of yourself first, before you help others. This is not selfish or wrong in any way. It's necessary.

Despite its importance, we really don't take self-care seriously. We all know instinctively how important self-care is, so why don't we do it? Why do we neglect our minds and bodies so much? Well, the neglect stops right here. We have an obligation to make a positive change in this world and there is no way that you will be able to spread love to others if you're stressed out and exhausted. You can't spend time or take care of loved ones if you're burned out. You can't be the best version of yourself if you don't take time for daily self-care.

The following are some of my favorite self-care practices:

Massage and Acupuncture

A massage from a professional or a friend or family member is so healing and feels great. Tension naturally builds up in the muscles on a daily basis and that is way more prevalent and hindering in people with anxiety. I personally love investing my money in things like massages. You'll start to realize your "return on investment" when your anxiety substantially decreases, you get better sleep, and you're able to relax consistently. Try and commit to a massage regularly. I know how expensive this can get, but you must get used to using your money for your healing. Don't forget, you can always ask a partner or a friend to give you one. I regularly give myself a foot massage with essential oils.

I also adore acupuncture. Acupuncture is a Chinese medicine technique that holds incredible healing powers. Your acupuncturist inserts tiny needles as thin as your hair into different points within the body. You then lie there with the needles in for about thirty minutes and the feeling is incredibly relaxing. I always feared needles and didn't overly enjoy my first few sessions, but after I faced the fear, I couldn't imagine life without acupuncture. You can literally feel the healing effects for days after your treatment. If you want to start small, or hate needles, you can also buy an acupressure mat. I lay on mine every night before bed.

The Relaxation Power of Stretches

Stretches are like free massages that you can give yourself daily. My massage therapist introduced me to the powerful healing of stretches. It is something I can do for my body when I can't get a massage. All I do is move my body around slowly and see when it tells me to stop and stretch. I slowly lean into the stretch and hold it. I like to hold my stretches for at least one minute. As I hold the stretch, I breathe deeply into it. The longer I hold the stretch, the further I can lean into it. I picture my inhales bringing in a calming breath to the area in which is tense. As I exhale, I release that tension in the muscles. Stretching has a powerful calming effect on both the mind and body. You can use yoga for stretching as well, or just do what I described above. I like to take 15 minutes a day to stretch. When I'm done, my body feels limp and relaxed.

Laughter

How often do you laugh? I want you to really think about this. We often go through our days without smiling or laughing often. Simply put, if we aren't laughing, we aren't living. I loved working at a public school for this very reason. Even though some days were draining to me, the kids were totally hilarious. I was laughing all the time. They really hold the key to laughter. Since children are just younger versions of ourselves, you can tap into that energy within yourself. Of course, what made us laugh as children may not work as well today, so adjust it. Go to a comedy club, watch a wildly inappropriate movie, and laugh your ass off. If you're not laughing regularly in your day, you need to restructure things. You need to start looking for opportunities to laugh. Start hiding behind corners and jumping out and scaring your friends and family members (don't do this to strangers or you may get arrested). You need to joke around a bit at work and lighten the mood. You have the power to bring laughter into your life. I'll take this opportunity to say something totally cliché here but, "laughter is your best medicine." It's the antidote to anxiety.

Grounding and Going Outside

In my experience, the best way to ground yourself is by going outside. It's important to ground yourself because we are so often chaotically jumbled in our heads. Practicing some grounding yoga poses, holding some stretches, or going outside brings healing.

There are companies that actually sell grounding mats that you can use inside your home, which may be a good option during the winter months, but the power of the earth on your bare feet really is something you can't replicate properly. Taking off your shoes and walking barefoot outside in the grass and dirt is incredibly healing. Don't be resistant to this. The outdoors has so many healing properties to the mind and body. Sounds too simplistic? Well, it is, and that's what makes it so effective for your healing process. We often expect solutions to be more complex than they actually are. The first time I heard this suggestion, I thought it was totally ridiculous. I remember thinking how the hell is this going to actually help me? However, as soon as I walked outside, I instantly felt my body become calm. It was almost as though my body was buzzing beforehand and as soon as I slipped those shoes off and placed them on the earth, my body started to relax and the buzzing stopped.

Getting Dressed

Again, as simplistic as this may sound, getting dressed is a great act of self-care. We can sometimes find ourselves in a rut, feeling depressed and sad. I've been there so many times, but getting dressed and having a shower will do wonders. Make a special effort during these times to choose clothes that make you feel good. Wash your face, look clean and fresh, and make yourself a priority. So often we neglect our looks and can start to feel run down and tired. When we put in that little extra effort to look good, it can help uplift our moods.

Socializing

Make a conscious choice to socialize more by carefully making a plan of WHO you are going to visit. I like to make a list of people who make me really happy. The people who, when I'm done visiting with them, make me smile and feel good long after I've left their presence. The people with whom, when I'm with them, I just laugh. You need this in your life. We all do. It's a human need to laugh and enjoy the company of others who make you feel loved, appreciated and overjoyed. I have so many amazing people on my list and when I don't see them enough, I know it's time to make plans.

This can be a trigger for many people with anxiety. We fear what others will think if we do, say, or act the wrong way and embarrass ourselves. We go through the fearful situations in our heads that talk us out of doing it. The truth is, it's healing to socialize with the RIGHT people. It's a basic human need to connect with others outside of the technology world. Having face-time (not apple) with people is essential and severely lacking in this day and age. That's why we have to consciously plan and be aware of this. If socializing seems too overwhelming right now, start small. Pick up the phone and hear a voice. See people in an environment that makes you comfortable. Shorten visit times by making plans before an appointment. That way your socializing visits are cut short, but you're still doing it. It's still a win, even if it's just for an hour. Choose to feed your *authentic mind* during this process and be kind to yourself.

Anxious or Negative Friends

Become aware of who you are spending your time with. This famous quote by Tim Ferriss is one of my favorites and he says "You are the average of the five people you most associate with." This is so very true. Think about when we were young and picked up habits or phrases our friends used all the time. I worked in the public school system for years and can't count the number of times little girls and boys mimicked the traits of their friends. We do the same as adults. A five-year-old will have a temper tantrum because she saw her friend get her way by doing so. An adult will pick up the habit of gossiping with their circle of friends when spending time with other gossipers. There is no difference here. Pay attention to how anxious and stressed you feel after spending time with certain people. This is something to keep in mind during your healing.

Setting Boundaries

As I've said before, try and stay away from the people and things that "sap" your strength and energy, at least until you're back on your feet again. You don't need to be mean, rude, or even short with these people. If they call, just ignore it and then send a quick text letting them know you will get in touch with them later. Little things like that can really help you get yourself back on track and connected with your *authentic self*. We must strongly consider cutting out or quitting the stuff that sucks our energy. The easy way to look at it is if it's not an excited "yes!" then it's, unfortunately, a "no." We have to begin to avoid people who are not necessarily going to make our day better and brighter by hanging out with them. We end up becoming a sponge for others' negativity. We can easily absorb others' stresses and pessimism. It's also very important not to judge them for it either. Judging them and becoming angry will not solve anyone's problems. Be the positive example and they will hopefully catch on and become that bright light themselves.

Sometimes in our recovery, we feel it may be necessary to set boundaries with these certain people in our lives. While this can often be true, do not set boundaries out of hurt and anger. Instead set boundaries out of love, patience and peace. So often I hear people say out of anger, "I have to set boundaries!" I am guilty of it myself. Sometimes we want to help others and when we feel that others are taking too much of us, we get angry at them. We don't want to take responsibility and realize that we have handed over too much of ourselves to them. We need to remember that when people are feeling desperate and someone helps them, they tend to not even realize they are asking or taking too much. It is OUR responsibility to know our limits and shut things down when we feel like we are becoming drained. It's wonderful to give to others and we should help and love one another, BUT we need to be very conscious of the signs where we are extending our hands out too far. That is when we lovingly have to forgive ourselves, as well as the people we feel are taking from us. Remember that you can't fake love, forgiveness, patience or peace. You actually have to feel it in your own heart for it to work. Don't forget that just because someone isn't doing something outright and obvious, doesn't mean they aren't sucking up your energy and draining you. Perhaps you only speak to someone once every few days but they are so negative all the time that you can't even handle those calls. You may not even have frequent interactions with them, but you still may need to set boundaries. Keep your antennas up for these things because the need to set boundaries applies to many different circumstances.

Get creative with your self-care. Make a point to laugh daily. Make your self-care enjoyable. Choose a better way of viewing your recovery and the world around you. The world is beautiful and filled with people who want to give you lots of love. It's not a scary place; it's a stunning world out there. Be grateful that you are here and honor your journey.

Chapter 10
Vacationing

Vacationing can be tricky with anxiety. We have great expectations for our vacations and hope so much that they will provide some reprieve from our everyday lives. We think and hope so much that if we could just get away, we could heal. Our anxiety will improve. When we arrive, however, it can sometimes be a very different story. Don't get me wrong, many people can easily vacation with anxiety. Sometimes, going on a vacation, away from the chronic stress of daily life, can be exactly what the doctor ordered. I have personally had many positive vacations as well as many negative experiences during my trips. It really depended heavily on what my life and mindset looked like before I left. We can't just expect our minds and bodies to all of a sudden slow down just because we decide it's vacation time. We need to prepare a few days in advance to get ourselves in the vacation mindset. I'll help give you some tips on how to do this.

First, take time to set an intention before your trip. Don't wait until you arrive at your destination to do this. Take a few days before you leave and talk about your intentions and expectations of the trip with your loved ones. Maybe your intention is to connect with your partner, read for hours on a beach or you want to get clear on some big upcoming decisions you need to make in your life. Setting that intention before you leave strengthens your *authentic mind*. It helps the other people who you are traveling with to understand what you want to do with your time. Ask them what their intentions for the trip are too. This way, everyone is on the same page. This sets the tone for success before you even leave. I always set an intention to let things roll off my shoulders more on vacations. Especially if something triggers or annoys me. I set the intention to let stuff go.

What people often don't understand is that it takes time to wind down. It sometimes can take a little longer than we'd hoped for. When we are "go, go, go," all the time, it's very difficult to just switch that off as soon as we hit the beach. It used to take me three days to even begin to wind down on vacation. By the time I began to wind down, it would be time to leave and I hated that. In fact, a good tell-tale sign that you have too much stress in your daily life is that it takes you two or three days to "come down" and relax on vacation. I am proud to say that I have now mastered vacationing. It only takes me a few hours to wind down these days but I had to practice this. It took me a few challenging vacations to note what I needed to work on and how I could quickly connect to my *authentic mind* and calm down.

I always start off my vacations with some sort of grounding process. This is where the "Five Senses of Peace" come in really handy. I often start my vacations off with this tool. It helps to re-focus my mind. Another grounding practice I love to do as soon as I arrive somewhere is take off my shoes and walk around on some grass to connect with nature. If this is not possible, I like to partake in an activity that has a grounding effect, like meditating in the hotel room for 15 minutes or swimming. I find 15 minutes to be the perfect amount of time for me to recalibrate myself back to peace. In fact, just forcing myself to be still for 15 minutes is exactly what can make or break a vacation for me.

Remember vacationing is not a time to be hard on yourself. You need to give yourself a break. Vacation time is not a time to be worrying about the little things. It's a time to let your hair down, not obsess about what to wear and just breathe in the new surroundings around you. It's a time to relish in the new place that you are in and discover cool new things. Get curious and allow your immaturity to run a bit wild. Embrace that childlike side. You must be easy on yourself. This is the time for that. If something doesn't go the way you had hoped or plans get scrambled around or changed, just accept it. At least you're on vacation and are taking a much needed break. We always have a choice to choose *anxious* or *authentic mind*, even when we are on vacation. You are the one who decides whether it will be a vacation filled with an attitude of frustration and disappointment or one of gratitude and excitement.

Another powerful activity I utilize at the beginning of a trip is to connect with other people. This doesn't mean you have to run up to some stranger on the beach and strike up a conversation. You can stop and have a friendly chat with the hotel staff or even with the people you are vacationing with. Stop, take a minute with your family and friends to chat and enjoy them. This is a good practice to do the first day you arrive. We tend to distract ourselves the first day of a vacation. With anxiety, we want to settle in and get ourselves feeling comfortable and safe first by unpacking and adjusting to our new environment. This can cause us some extra anxiety because new environments feel unsafe to us. Be kind and patient with yourself through this transition. It may take you a little extra time to become relaxed and comfortable. Take this time to connect with other people with love in your heart. If you haven't noticed yet, people on vacation are a lot friendlier and are in a much better mood. Take advantage of this. Pray that everyone, even the strangers around the pool, can all have fun, relax, and have peace. Redirecting your focus onto others can have a powerful grounding effect. Vacations are also an amazing time to strengthen your spiritual practice. I always set the intention to strengthen my spiritual practice during these times. It helps to keep things in perspective for me and allows me to rest and connect to my *authentic self* much quicker than anything else.

Something else I wanted to touch on here is switching your routine up. Often when we revisit the same vacation spots, we have heavy expectations based on our previous visits. We always feel the need to compare. Was this time better than the last time? If you find yourself doing this, try not to recreate the moment and control your vacations. I used to always have a strict routine when visiting my favorite places. My *anxious mind* would take over. I'd check in, unpack and go for a swim. Then I'd go to the same restaurant for dinner. I always tried to recreate the many wonderful times I had before. I figured that if I did the same things and followed the same routines, that I'd experience the feelings I had before. The problem with that is you can't recreate moments because they are not about circumstances, they are about feelings. When you feel intense joy and peace, it's not because you're sitting in a certain place or going to a certain restaurant. Yes, you may be reminded of the feelings you had but all the mind really wants is to experience those feelings again. Frankly, it wasn't until I switched things up and began to have different and unique experiences that I was really able to truly let go and enjoy myself.

One thing that used to happen to me on every trip was that I would get the "last-day-blues." I would get sad and depressed on the last day. A trick that helped me during these times was to remember that it's not my last experience and be grateful for what the trip brought me. Also, when I returned home, I would not talk about the trip with people who weren't supportive, happy and excited for me. After your trip, continue to live on the high. Allow the remnants of the trip to radiate from you. Relish in the joy you experienced. Get excited about going home and for your new-found love and peace that you will share with others.

Releasing Expectations

I want to talk about releasing expectations in the context of vacationing because it really applied to me whenever I tried to rest or take a break. Releasing expectations can literally be applied to every single area of your life including relationships and careers. Vacations were a specifically stressful time for me. The main reason for this was because of the expectations I put on myself and the trip. I'm sure we've all experienced this at some point. You really look forward to something and it just doesn't deliver. Sometimes, and in my case most of the time, we actually sabotage our experiences. As an anxiety sufferer, panic and anxiety attacks can really increase on vacations. I always wondered why this would happen. How could something I loved so much become such a trigger for me? Was I that far down the road that even my vacations were triggering me now? What was wrong with me? This pattern continued over and over again. When I finally brought this problem to my own coach's attention, we talked in depth about vacations and expectations. She helped me realize the reason as to why I was so triggered. It was because I was going in with so much pressure on myself and so many expectations. Expectations really equal pressure. When we always have expectations, we don't allow the beauty and spontaneity of life to take over. We miss out on all the magic. When I was able to adopt a more casual outlook on vacations and release the expectations, the outcomes became amazing. The "should mentality" is controlling. We often get hung up on how things "should" work out or happen. When I'm using "should" too often, I know my expectations are out of control and need to be released. With OCD, I always tend to really fixate on outcomes, as I'm sure many of you do too. I couldn't seem to release them or get them out of my head.

My spiritual relationship helped me because I truly believed that God had my back. When you feel the power and support from something greater than yourself and believe that everything happens for a reason, releasing "should haves" and expectations becomes a lot easier and a hell of a lot more effective. If you believe everything works out for the good, you really have nothing to fear.

When I practiced this, the outcomes always turned out better than I could have thought or imagined. That's what you have to do sometimes. Release the outcomes and expectations. The outcomes are often so much better when we don't have these thoughts and heavy expectations attached to them.

Chapter 11
Overstimulation and Anxiety

We crave simplicity.

Our bodies and minds crave unplugging the phone, turning off the TV and going outside. We crave peace and are nostalgic because we grew up in a simpler time. As a society, we are so hungry for calm, but we don't even know where to start to find it. We try and feed that hunger with other things, but in doing so we are never satisfied. We tend to feel like something is "off" but can't quite put our finger on it. We blame other things in our lives for this "off" feeling and think if we change them, life will be different and better. The truth is, if you're trying to search for something outside of what you really need, you will never be satisfied. In our hunger for peace and our failure to find it, we focus on what we can do to distract and overstimulate ourselves.

The American Psychological Association claims that millennials experience more stress and are less able to manage it than any other generation. So, the big question is, why do millennials seem to have a higher rate of anxiety and depression more than any other generation? Well, one reason is time. We have a bit of an obsession with it and are very impatient. This is something that I mainly blame on the recent warp-speed advancements in technology over the last ten years or so. In the last five years alone, I've seen a huge shift in happiness amongst so many people. First, we have TV streaming programs like Netflix, so we spend our time watching a lot more TV, binging if you will, and not enough time outside or socializing with friends.

Next, we have the "superphone." The introduction of the "superphone" has quickly changed everything. We are all privy to the massive amounts of information about the damages of overusing your phone. We know it's bad, but we do it anyways. I'd love to tell you that I never overuse my phone, but I can't. When you're bored, it's easy to just grab your phone. When we are waiting in line, we don't even have to go through the awkward silences, small talk, or coming up with interesting things to say. We just reach into our pockets and grab our phones. The awkward silence may be gone, but so are our abilities to use our social skills. The worst part about it is, not only are we mindlessly scrolling down our social media pages and not using our actual social skills, but we are also exposing our eyes and brains to more electric and magnetic fields (EMFs). This seriously messes with our mind and nervous system.

Social media is great for keeping in touch with old friends and looking at pictures of family members who you would otherwise never see. When social media began to really gain its popularity back in 2005, I remember thinking how cool it was to be able to see all these pictures and connect with friends I had lost touch with over the years. It seemed like such a blessing, but unfortunately it has become very addictive. Even though there are many wonderful aspects to it, we have to watch the unhealthy habits it reinforces. When you suffer from anxiety or depression, it is common to withdraw from social situations. Social media has made this even easier to do because anxiety and depression sufferers can now feel safe to stay at home and scroll through their pages. This provides an artificial feeling that we are still experiencing life by looking through others' pictures and posts. We also have free support groups on platforms such as Facebook, which allow us to connect with people suffering from anxiety and depression too. This is all great and a wonderful way to connect with others; however, we must proceed with caution.

Some of these groups can actually severely hinder us. Finding a commonality of suffering isn't always good. It can reinforce our pain and convince us that we have no choice in our suffering and are doomed to struggle with these issues forever. I will never forget reading an article online when I was trying to heal. The article was titled, "Things You Should Never Say to Someone with Anxiety." As I can appreciate the message the author of this blog was trying to make, I couldn't help but think how damaging these types of articles can be. We see things like this and they tattoo themselves into our psyche. They make us think that we cannot choose *authentic thoughts* over *anxious thoughts*. These articles keep us stuck in a victim mentality and tell us that the world should adapt to our anxiety, which is completely unrealistic and setting us up for total failure. We then form expectations of the people around us and when they fail to accommodate us, we get upset and hurt. We tell them they don't care about us. This just further separates us from one another, thus making recovery more difficult. We must use social media in a productive and healthy way or else we may be hindering our recovery more than we think. It is still a form of media, so become savvy about the messages you receive.

I remember six years ago when I married my husband, the world was a different place. We didn't all have data plans on our phones as "the norm." Hell, I didn't even have a touch screen yet. I am grateful that I had my wedding a few years ago, so no one was scrolling through their phones during the ceremony. Everyone was present and we literally had the most magical day, surrounded by the ones we loved. It felt like it was right out of a movie. We laughed and got bored waiting for the photographers, so we killed time by talking to one another and joking around. That's the beauty of human connection. The more we lose it, the more we long for it and crave it, yet the problem is, we don't know what we are craving and missing. It's slipping away from us so quickly, yet so subtlety. We don't even realize it's happening. Instead, we have a whirlwind of technology and overstimulation around us that we don't have time to assess. Our solution is to reach into our pockets and grab our phones to distract us from our fears, worries, and even dreams that we allow to slip away.

Now, here's a shocking fact: Television binging actually stresses you out.

When streaming programs came out, we were all so excited. I'm personally a huge fan. I think it's a great advancement in our world. I love watching shows this way, so I'm not saying it's a bad thing. However, we need to become aware of the facts in order to heal and binge watching is not good for anxiety. We often associate it with winding down or "chilling." There are many reasons as to why binging on shows is harmful to our anxiety. First of all, it teaches our brains to be impatient. We no longer need to wait for commercials or next episodes to come out. This reinforces the belief that everything in life should be instantaneous. We don't condition ourselves to be patient. Our brains, instead, have actually been trained to be incredibly impatient. Patience is a very important skill to have, especially in healing anxiety. It's one we need to practice diligently.

Another point is that as far as our anxiety goes, it's not good for our bodies to physically sit still for that long. This is not as much of an issue after a long day at work when you just want to rest your feet. This is more of an issue when spending a whole Saturday on the couch. When our bodies are still for too long and our eyes are fixated on a blue light giving off EMF's, it can really elevate our anxiety. This increases our cortisol and makes anxiety worse. We also tend to not fully listen to the TV shows after a while anyways. They are usually just on in the background of our *anxious* thoughts. We use TV as a way to rest, unwind, and distract ourselves, but really we are still thinking the *anxious* thoughts anyways. Depending on the show, we can even get triggered by the things we see, without even being aware of it. For example, you may see someone on the screen getting diagnosed with an illness, or you see a husband cheating on his wife. To those of us constantly thinking from our *anxious minds*, we tend to hold on to those negative images and start to think about them over and over again.

Don't get me wrong. I binge watch from time to time, and I scroll through my phone when I'm bored. This is why I've noticed it becoming such a huge problem with this generation and society in general. This is not something to panic about or feel like you need to make huge changes right away. In fact, jumping from one extreme to the next just causes more anxiety and discomfort. The point of this chapter is to make you become aware of these issues. To admit there is a problem and in order to conquer anxiety, you will need to address it. Even though your mom or grandparents had anxiety during a technology free age, there are still more contributing factors that cause anxiety in modern society. One of the biggest factors is the increased use of media and technology. We are exposed to so many messages, light, and speed that we don't even know how to connect to our true selves, minds or bodies.

It is our responsibility to stay focused in the midst of all this electronic change, and we need to remember there are addictive patterns in this behavior. Learn when to unplug. Stop taking pictures of that beautiful sunset and actually LOOK at the damn sunset! Yes, pictures are wonderful, but what's more important are the actual memories. We put too much emphasis on material things.

We live in a world that is always looking for what's to come next. Multi-tasking is now fully accepted as being normal that it's actually expected of us. Normal now means that we must be insanely busy and overwhelmed by life. Relaxing is nearly impossible with our TVs streaming in the background while we send text messages, check the weather, and read our e-mails. These things are all incredibly easy to access, so we need to proceed with caution.

How can we expect our children to be calm, go to bed at 8pm, and sleep through the night, when we have no idea how to do it for ourselves? We need light silence, sound silence, and stimulation silence. As our social skills are diminishing, our knowledge of technology is quickly building, yet we are all feeling lost. We have disconnected from life, nature and God. We need a media detox, so we don't miss our lives and memories. If you took that urge that you have to pick up your phone as a cue that you need to take some deep breaths, connect with yourself and relax, the results would be pretty transformational.

In the same way we plug our phones and electronics in to recharge at night, we need to do the opposite as human beings. We charge *our* batteries by *unplugging* from all forms of technology. It's not enough to unplug when we go to bed at night. We need more of a break throughout the day. So lose the cell phone and the iPad for a few hours when you're particularly anxious.

Don't dismiss other forms of stimulation here either. There are many ways in which we are overstimulated and it's not all technology's fault. We overstimulate ourselves with food, drugs, and alcohol too. You'll actually meet people in your life who don't know what to do with themselves unless they are stimulated by something 24/7. These people are craving peace more than anyone else. We often overstimulate our minds with things that hold no true benefit because we are under-stimulated in the areas that matter. For example, you may be under-stimulated at your job.

You've been there for years, and you've lost your passion for it. You go home and try and numb yourself by overstimulating your senses with technology, addictions, or food. Or perhaps you feel under-stimulated in your relationships. Whatever it may be, look into it. You may be surprised at what you find. Simplifying our lives is the key here. I give you some great tips on how to do that at the end of this chapter.

Journal Break

How can we detox from media? Think about a few things that have worked and can work for you and write it in your journal.

Some great strategies that I have used for my media detoxes are as follows:

- Take one day a week and dedicate the entire day to making a conscious choice to stay off your technology as often as possible. I like to use these days to connect with nature and with people.

- Start small if you must. Like other addictions, technology use is an addiction too and should be treated as such. So switch up your routine with your technology. If every day you come home, sit on your couch and watch TV or go on your cell phone, take 30 of those minutes and use one of these alternate strategies instead.

- "Hit the ground!" When I'm on my phone too much, I tell myself to hit the ground immediately and meditate. I may hold some stretches and deep breaths here too. Telling myself to hit the ground has this immediate effect on me and I stay on the ground until I can stand up relaxed.

- Get grounded. Here I like to do some balancing yoga poses or go outside, kick off my socks and shoes and walk around barefoot in the grass. This has an intense relaxing effect on the body.

- Use this time to journal.

- Move your body. You don't need a massive, sweaty workout here. In fact, a walk outside will usually do the trick. The gym can be good too, but outside is much, much better.

- Pamper yourself. Run a bath, but practice it. Practice having a bath? Yup! Relaxation and pampering ourselves doesn't really come easily, but it's something enjoyable to practice. Like everything else, it gets much easier with consistency.

- Read - just make sure it's on paper. We talk a lot about the blue light that radiates off of our devices. You need a rest from that. Read a paperback instead.

- Get creative. I used to love buying blank canvases and painting on them, even though I have no artistic ability whatsoever. It really doesn't matter here. Creativity is healing. Play music, draw or write. Experiment with what feels exciting for you.

- Listen to some music. I don't have to tell you how therapeutic music is. It can switch up what we are focusing on and move us very quickly from a negative state into a positive state.

- Listen to personal development. You can use your phone for this, but I don't want you on your technology mindlessly scrolling through social media platforms. I will often pop on an audio of a guided meditation or listen to some of my favorite speakers. It's vital to our development to listen to people who are where we want to be. You may as well listen to the people who have already accomplished the goals you have. Who better to teach than someone who has been through it and come out on the other side?

Reducing time spent overstimulating ourselves with technology and other addictions will accelerate your healing. It's pretty cool to watch your anxiety transform by making these simple changes. We will actually apply some of these technology detox strategies during the 40 Day Program at the end of the book. Just remember, at times, recovery from anxiety may feel overwhelming. When you're feeling overwhelmed, just ask yourself, is this process more overwhelming than the anxiety itself? Sometimes these changes may feel like too much but we must immerse ourselves in positive change in order to condition our brains away from anxiety and closer to peace.

Section Two
"Break a Leg:" Chemical Imbalances

As I spoke about earlier, each section in this book is created to weaken each leg of "The Tripod of Anxiety." One by one we will help dismantle each leg. The following section focuses on chemical imbalances and tools we can use to help.

Chapter 12

Our Bodies, Our Health and Our Anxiety

Our bodies are wildly complex and fascinating. What I have found even more fascinating in recent years is the mind and body connection. It's fascinating how our thoughts have more of an impact on our health than we think. We can decide to make our body our worst enemy or our best friend. There's a good chance that if you hate your body, your body fights you right back. Your body knows if you hate it or if you love it. It knows if you are frustrated with it, or if you're at peace with it. I've tested this theory out so many times, and I know it to be true. When your mind sends your body negative messages, your body responds to them. Whenever I felt as though I hated my body and was fed up, my health always got worse. My lymph glands would swell, my body would swell, I would feel sick and totally exhausted.

This is why it's so essential to love our bodies. If you're not sure whether you love your body or not, then you probably don't. I say this because we are bombarded by constant negative and comparative messages about the body on a daily basis. We are conditioned to be unsatisfied with our bodies and to get angry and frustrated when we experience pain. We compare our bodies to other bodies and even receive messages from other people that our bodies aren't good enough. What we have to understand is that our body is our business and nobody else's.

The *anxious mind* has a natural talent of knowing exactly how to attack the body, yet we can make a choice here. We can decide whether we listen to the *anxious mind's* opinion of our body or the *authentic mind's* opinion. Challenge yourself for one week to only choose thoughts from your *authentic mind* when it comes to your body. If someone comments about your body, tell them that your body is only your business. Then, forgive them for it and move on. The *anxious mind* loves to keep you negative and sick, while the *authentic mind* knows the true healing potential of the body and wants you to know it too.

Journal Break

How would you describe your relationship with your body? Do you love it or loath it? Remember that our body's purpose is not to just sit around all day and be judged by you and others. The purpose of the body is to love and support us in all our life's dreams and endeavors. Do "The Five Senses of Peace" right now, but have the focus be on your body.

When we experience things in life such as trauma, our brains and bodies can actually rewire themselves. This can cause harmful imbalances within the body, and as a result, we can become sick. Sick meaning mental illnesses too. On the other hand, our bodies can just as easily repair and heal themselves in incredible ways. We are incredibly intricate. Our brains can literally teach our body to heal or to get sicker. This little transaction between the brain and the body can actually happen quite quickly too. If you've experienced trauma, then you know what I'm talking about. The term "fight or flight" is used when your body is under extreme stress, panic, or danger. Your brain sends messages to the rest of your body to do something about it in order to try and stop it and prevent it from ever happening again. Out of all of the clients that

I have worked with, there hasn't been one yet that hasn't experienced some form of trauma. Those traumatic experiences not only bring anxiety, but they can cause chemical imbalances in the brain that can trigger mental illness and disease. The good news is that we can rewire and reprogram them to support us, not sabotage us.

Intuition and Tuning into Your Body and Mind

You are your own best doctor.

You actually know what is best for your health. We were created that way. Our bodies are miracles that were constructed with an intuitive mind that actually knows what is good for us and what isn't. Before doctors existed, humans intuitively knew what was good and what was bad for their heath. We have been constructed with these amazing mechanisms within the body with the sole purpose of protecting and healing us. We all have such unique chemical and bodily balances that are specific to us. Everybody is different, and every body is different. Meaning, there is no way a doctor can heal twenty sick bodies with similar symptoms the same way. Instead of treating each person as an individual with unique balances within the body, doctors automatically turn to pharmaceuticals to heal all bodily woes. They don't have time to look at our unique cases. Pills are quick and easy. We take these pills, yet deep down, we know that pharmaceuticals are mostly a Band-Aid that are not going to solve our root issues. That is why it is so important for us to focus on our intuition, so we can tune into our bodies, know what is right or wrong, and know how to fix it. Only we know what is best for us. Our natural state of being is knowing intuitively what to do and what to avoid.

Your body and health must be number one. As anxiety sufferers, we can tend to adopt some unhealthy habits or take medications that damage our bodies. If we intuitively feel as if we need those medications right now as a temporary relief, we have to be incredibly careful about how we treat our bodies the rest of the time. Since pharmaceuticals of any kind put extra stress on the body, we must compensate by being extra kind to our bodies. We have to understand that anxiety sufferers tend to cut corners on our health. We tend to feel guilty when we put our health first, even if that guilt is on a subconscious level. That feeling must come to an end if you want to heal. The good news is there are tons of things we can do to help restore our bodies, if we feel like our bodies are in disarray. The body is so resilient and heals itself easier than you may think. I've been personally amazed by what my body has gone through and how it has healed itself time and time again. The body wants to repair itself back to its natural state, but it needs our help. It is up to us to work on our thoughts about our health and bodies. We must make up new rules for ourselves that totally support our health restoration. I now make up my own rules when it comes to what's healthy for me or not, and I believe that to be the key to healing. Some days, I may feel like I need that extra vitamin and some days I may feel like it's too much. I make the choices. That's what tuning into your body looks like. Some days, my body wants a cupcake because it's healing for my soul. Some days, it wants only greens with no meat at all.

Intuition is going with your gut. We've all said it before, "I've got a bad feeling about this." Anxiety sufferers seem to get bad feelings about many things. How do we distinguish between *anxious mind* and *authentic mind* when it comes to intuition? One of our "super powers" as anxiety sufferers is that we have stronger levels of intuition accuracy. This means that the accuracy of our gut reactions is more accurate than those of others. Our minds are naturally wired this way. So, instead of using this special talent for good, the *anxious mind* often uses it for bad. We use this intuition to over-analyze and obsess about outcomes, and we worry to the extreme. If only we used this to feed our *authentic mind,* we could actually heal ourselves faster.

So again, how do we know if our intuition comes from the *anxious mind* or *the authentic mind?* The answer is simple. It's right if it feels good. If it's not a "hell yes," then it's a "no." The more you start to heal from anxiety, the more you will notice this intuition align with your *authentic mind,* and it will become stronger. You will start to base your choices and decisions on this strong talent that we have. Now, obviously logic comes into play in certain situations, but the more you start to tune into your mind and body, your mind will naturally start feeling intuition stronger.

Another way I like to distinguish between my *anxious mind's* intuition and my *authentic mind's* is that I ask myself this question, "Does this choice come from fear or love?" You will know the difference. When I went to my first acupuncture session, I cried the entire time. It was uncomfortable at first and I was terrified of needles. When I came home that night, I decided I would never go back again. It wasn't for me. Then something strange happened. I went to bed that night and the next morning when I woke up, I announced to my husband that I was going back to acupuncture. I swear his jaw hit the floor. He was so shocked since my first appointment appeared to be so difficult for me. I then explained to him that something inside of me wanted to return. I told him if I never went back, I knew I was making that health choice out of fear and I had to face it. I also just knew that my acupuncturist had healing hands. I knew this in my core - if I wanted to get better, I had to go back. It turned out to be one of the most healing experiences of my entire life. I faced the fear and now thoroughly enjoy my acupuncture appointments.

I've also had experiences in my health journey where I made choices out of fear and truly wish I hadn't. When I was only fifteen years old I was put on a pill called Diane 35. I was hesitant at first because it initially made me gain a lot of weight, as well as made me feel very sick and nauseous. I wasn't feeling great physically and began to get severely depressed. This pill, however, was clearing up my teenage acne, which was something I was incredibly insecure about. So I stayed on that pill for thirteen years. This was my doctor's solution to a hormonal disorder that I had developed. I would constantly ask my doctor if it was safe. He always assured me it was. As the years went on, I started hearing details about this pill. I heard of other girls around the world who were beginning to develop severe health issues from it. I asked my doctor again, and he said it was fine. I would remind him how long I had been on it and he constantly assured me it was fine. He also told me that all of my previous health issues would return if I stopped taking the pill. Of course, I didn't want that to happen, so I stayed on it. Then I started to have these numbness episodes. I was waking up in the middle of the night grabbing my chest and gasping for air while my entire body, head to toe was going numb. I knew something was wrong, but I didn't know the cause.

Finally, after being on it for so long, I came across this article online about the pill I was on. The article provided information about all these girls around the world experiencing heart attacks and strokes from Diane 35. Some of these girls had this reaction after only four months. Therefore, the pill was banned in Europe and the U.S. yet was still available in Canada. This was my little nod from God, that gave me the extra push to stop taking the pills now. I quickly made an appointment with my doctor and brought this to his attention. What was his response? "Stay on the pill." I couldn't believe what I was hearing. I went home and that day started slowly weaning myself off of it.

During the weaning process, I experienced several situations that landed me in the hospital with life-threatening, stroke-like symptoms. I've never experienced anything like it in my life. After several episodes, I decided to just stop the pill altogether. It was a choice that saved my life. The episodes stopped.

I was not great at listening to my body back then. I stayed on the pill for fear that my body would go into complete disarray if I didn't. I didn't listen to my *authentic mind* until I finally decided to stop.

The pill changed the biochemistry in my body. It took years for me to heal after this health crisis. The funny thing about this story is that I knew something was wrong inside of my body for years but never knew how to trust or tune into it. I trusted my doctor and didn't trust myself. I learned a valuable lesson from that experience. Doctors are humans. Their schooling and the medical profession promotes a place for pharmaceutical companies to sell their drugs as a treatment. They are not a treatment. We are our own best doctors. We need to be proactive when it comes to our health and stop accepting things at face value just because it comes from a doctor.

Physical Symptoms

Sometimes anxiety can give us some serious physical symptoms. Anyone who has ever been through a panic attack knows this. I remember my first one. I was in school. My ears clogged up completely and I couldn't hear anything but a faint little beeping sound. My body instantly became soaked with sweat and all the color drained from my face. The room began to get cloudy and I actually passed out. I woke up, sick to my stomach and feeling so tired that I had to leave school.

Next time you convince yourself that anxiety doesn't take its toll on your body, remember that story.

I'll never forget the time I was experiencing intense physical symptoms from a severe concussion. I remember walking around trying to enjoy myself on a nice Saturday with my husband, but I was struggling. I kept telling myself to try and live in the moment and take a relaxing breath, but I couldn't do it. All I could focus on was the fear. My *anxious mind* wouldn't stop that day. I feared that my head was permanently damaged. The more I feared, the worse it became. I was obsessing, and I couldn't stop. As I was getting increasingly dizzy and foggy, I couldn't shut off my terrifying thoughts. My husband was trying to talk me through my panic, helping me in any way he knew how. Still, my symptoms got worse.

As we were walking down the street, we ran into my brother-in-law and his friend. It's funny how those situations pop up. All of a sudden, I was totally re-directed. I was completely shocked and happy to see them both. We started hugging, laughing, and talking. For the moment, I was no longer focused on my head. I wasn't focused on the fogginess or the fear of being permanently brain damaged. Instead, I was forced to socialize. As we continued to talk, they invited us to go to the karaoke bar they were headed to. I was nervous to go because I knew how much worse my concussion symptoms were getting and I feared the loud bar would set me back even further in my recovery, but I decided to go anyways. All four of us got a table, sat down and started talking. As we were sitting and talking in this extremely loud karaoke bar, I started to really enjoy myself. In fact, for about 15 minutes, I totally forgot about my head and found myself laughing as my husband got up to sing. The night went on, and we ended up dancing, joking, and having the best time. It wasn't until then that

I realized that for a full two hours, I was totally symptom-free. The dizziness, fogginess, fears, and worries had all slipped away.

Anxiety tricks you.

It can actually fool you so bad that it can manifest itself into very real, physical symptoms. It's kind of a way for your *anxious mind* to prove that it's right, you're doomed, and there's nothing you can do about it - more lies your mind tells you. The good news is that we can repair the body. The body is programmed to fix and repair itself. It wants to work with you to heal. So keep your eyes open for these moments and symptoms. I can promise you that once your *anxious mind* begins to diminish in power, the symptoms will too.

Chapter 13
Healing the Body

We know the body wants to heal, feel safe, and return to its natural state of excellent health. The body actually always works hard to repair itself, twenty four hours a day, seven days a week. It works hard to detox, to keep a healthy balance, and to heal wounds both internally and externally. That's where our minds come into play. They become our greatest healing tool. We can decide whether we want to fight against this natural healing process or work with it to help the body heal faster. Make the choice today to heal your thoughts so that your body's healing soon follows.

I must explain that the information in this chapter has worked in my personal healing journey. It's not meant to replace advice from a qualified medical practitioner. I'm just sharing the information I have come across in my research and personal experiences. I will always encourage you to make your own choices regarding your health care based on your own research and experiences. The following are some amazing ways in which we can tune in, listen, and give the body what it wants in order to heal.

My Magnesium Rant

You may have read about magnesium before and possibly shrugged it off as just another mineral, but what you may not know is that magnesium and anxiety have an uncanny connection. Correcting a magnesium deficiency has actually eliminated anxiety disorders in some people.

Magnesium is not just a beneficial mineral, it's essential for every part of your body to function properly, especially the nervous system and brain. It is essential to over 700 different enzyme systems. Without adequate magnesium to moderate the adrenal glands, the fight or flight hormones are easily triggered, which can cause elevated heart rate and anxiety attacks. Not only do we need it to feel good and function, but an underlying magnesium deficiency can be the root cause for major diseases including heart disease, cancer, diabetes and so much more.

So why are we so deficient? Why is this SUCH a huge problem, especially in people with anxiety and depression? Well, magnesium runs out of our bodies very quickly, especially during times of stress. The body uses tons of magnesium while it produces and moderates stress hormones. On top of that, our soils and foods are so depleted that you can't possibly eat enough nuts or greens to replenish your lost magnesium stores. If you have anxiety problems, it's almost impossible NOT to be somewhat magnesium deficient. Why? It's due to the constant stress our bodies are under. When we are stressed or even worried about something, our bodies suck up magnesium faster than a new vacuum. It is THE stress mineral. If you take anxiety meds, anti-depressants, birth control pills or almost any prescription or nonprescription drug, these drugs massively deplete your magnesium. If you smoke, drink, work out a lot and sweat, your precious magnesium is significantly reduced. We aren't taking in nearly as much magnesium as we are pumping out. That's a huge problem for our bodies. It depletes us and gives us more anxiety, depression, and disease.

The list of magnesium deficiency symptoms is a long one. People often turn to painkillers, antidepressants, cannabis and even thyroid medications for their underlying magnesium deficiencies, because they start to feel aches and pains, get insomnia, and feel as though their bodies need more support. The problem with turning to these other "treatments" is that they aren't correcting the deficiency itself, so you may find temporary relief from your symptoms, but when you stop taking them, the symptoms will return. People are often using these meds for an underlying magnesium deficiency because the symptoms are the same. That is why it is always necessary to correct this deficiency first.

My experience with this miracle mineral is pretty amazing. With my OCD diagnosis at such a young age, I dealt with high levels of stress my entire life. I hid it well, which put even more stress on my body. I never replenished my magnesium other than from a multi Flintstones vitamin that my mother made me eat every day, which I now realize did absolutely nothing. As I got older, I would work out, go into saunas, take anti-anxiety meds, and do a hell of a lot of other magnesium-depleting stuff on a regular basis. I took prescription meds as well. I ended up in the hospital with electrolyte failure and no one, not even the doctors, knew what was happening to me. I always drank tons of plain water and stayed away from salt because I thought it was bad for me (table salt is but pink salt or any sea salt is actually essential for us). Drinking water is great, but if you drink too much plain water, it can actually flush magnesium out of your body. Adding a healthy salt to your water can help combat this.

Another part of the magnesium deficiency epidemic is that the standard magnesium blood tests are inaccurate. They almost always come out normal and these are false "normal" readings. We actually have to ask our doctors for a specialized, accurate test. They are missing the problem and giving patients completely wrong advice and treatment. The serum magnesium test, which is the standard test doctors use for magnesium, only measures the small amount of magnesium floating around in your blood and is not measuring the amount that is in your cells or your stores. So not only are these tests inaccurate, but they are actually dangerous. This is because they give you false "normal" readings, allowing millions of severely undiagnosed magnesium deficiencies to slip by.

For an accurate check on where your magnesium levels are in your body, go to your doctor and request an RBC (Red Blood Cell) magnesium test. Don't be surprised if your doctor makes a passive aggressive comment when you ask for it! This test will cost you around 50 dollars, but it could save your life. Deaths from heart attacks and even cancer, could likely have been caused by a severe magnesium deficiency.

Another reason why magnesium deficiency is such an epidemic is the fact that magnesium is very difficult to replenish because it is not very absorbable within the body. The body doesn't digest magnesium pills very well. In fact, we absorb a small amount from the pill form of magnesium.

So, what is the solution to this massive problem? Needless to say, we need more magnesium. The good news is that it's fixable. One of the best ways to get your levels up is transdermal or topical magnesium. It has been proven to bring RBC magnesium levels up faster than many other methods because it bi-passes the digestive system. The first thing you can do is go buy quality magnesium oil or gel. It has been known to tingle or burn a bit in some people. Know that if it burns a little that it doesn't mean you should stop using it. Your skin adjusts in about a week or so and you can also wash the gel off your body after thirty minutes. This doesn't mean to stop taking the oral magnesium pills either. It's good to cover all your bases when trying to get your levels up.

By far the best form of magnesium is picometer magnesium. This is a cellular magnesium that gets your levels us fast. It is the most highly absorbable form of this mineral. Nothing can replace the effectiveness of picometer, but picometer is not popular; thus, it must be ordered online in most cases. My personal favorite product is called ReMag. Remag is named "The Magnesium Miracle" and it is just that. It was created by the magnesium queen herself, Dr. Carolyn Dean, and is the most effective product I've seen for bringing up magnesium levels. You can put it in your water, as this is liquid magnesium. Magnesium chloride is also a wonderful, absorbable form. It is usually sold in individual packages at the health food store in a powder form. If you use magnesium chloride, you should also be doing a topical magnesium daily until your levels are up.

When you finally get your magnesium levels up, you will experience an extremely relaxing effect on the mind and body. You may not experience this relaxing effect until you restore your levels and it may even give you some energy at the beginning, but trust me when I say, being diligent with magnesium daily is a must for healing.

Getting your RBC test done every three to four months is so important too, as you want to really keep track and monitor how your body is reacting to your dose. Getting regular blood work until your body is at an ideal saturation level is vital. RBC magnesium is measured differently in every country, so when your results come in, make sure to ask your doctor what the system of measure is. Your ideal levels on your RBC should be as follows, depending on the country you live in:

4.2 - 6.9 (mg/dL) or 2.4 - 2.6 (mmol/L) or 3.37 - 5.77 (mEq/L)

If your levels aren't within these ranges, you need to replenish. Remember to stop all magnesium supplements a day before your blood test to get an accurate reading, which includes the topical oil and gel. Magnesium is very safe and you can use it on your whole family to avoid deficiency. Be patient. It can take up to a year to properly restore chronically low magnesium levels. If you're severely deficient, like I was, the changes in your mind and body will be subtle, but one day you will wake up and notice how much better you feel overall. This could possibly be one of the most life changing and life-saving things you take away from this book. Like everything else in this book, diligence and patience will become your two best friends. Be happy that you're healing, stay in the *authentic mind*, and be grateful for every level of healing in both body and mind.

Foods that Heal

Whether you want to hear it or not, fruits and vegetables are the most healing foods on the planet. We instinctively know which foods heal and which ones don't. We have been told to avoid sugar, even natural sugars, which is just a trend in my opinion. I personally followed this trend and decided to cut out all sugar for two years, including fruits, and by the end of that time I felt sicker than I ever felt before. When I finally gave into my natural sugar craving, I started shoveling fruit into my body. My body knew it was starving for the unique nutrients that only fruit can provide. My body started to instantly feel amazing. It felt as though I hadn't drank any water for a week and finally found a clean crisp stream to drink from. Complete relief. Instant healing. My blood tests improved very quickly after I re-introduced fruit. That's when I knew I had to pass this information on.

There is actually a wonderful book written by Anthony Williams on this topic called, "Life Changing Foods" and I can promise you that it will make you fall in love with eating healthy. After reading this book, I swear all you want to do is go out and buy beautiful, healing fruit. Anthony also speaks on the power of juicing. Juicing fresh fruits and vegetables is probably the most healing thing I ever did for my body. You can literally feel the nutrients vibrating inside of your cells after drinking one fresh juice. Juicers can be a bit pricey but are literally worth every penny. Blenders just don't do what a juicer can do. There is something about juicing that is healing, period. Try it out, you will feel it instantly.

I'm not going to tell you which foods to avoid, you know that already. Every body is different and some bodies love things like grains and meat while others hate them. You know what your body likes and what it hates. These things can also change from day to day. I notice that when I eat too much unnatural sugar, I can feel worse as far as my anxiety goes. However, some days my body just wants a damn doughnut and I feel great afterwards. The reason I won't tell you what foods are good for you and what foods are bad for you is because I don't really believe in it. I don't believe in a one-size fits all diet. I believe in unique diets for unique individuals. One thing I truly believe is that limiting and restricting yourself of any pleasure all the time is not wise for anxious people. Everything in moderation is the key. There will be times when a rainbow ice cream on a hot day brings you so much joy, that it's healthier for your body than a salad. Sometimes the chemicals, such as dopamine, released into the brain from truly enjoying your food are better for your body than actual healthy food. There is an obvious balance here for sure, but it's true. I've literally felt better on vacation eating more unhealthy foods than when I was at home eating my strictly regimented, doctor prescribed diet. My skin would glow, I'd have more energy, and just be plain happier. Some of us need to be on a specific diet for health reasons, and I'm not at all suggesting throwing that away, but I am asking you to give yourself a break sometimes. Listen to your body and tune in.

Food mainly becomes a problem when it's used as a replacement for emotion or when it's used to calm or comfort the body. Sometimes we have no idea how to feel our feelings or comfort ourselves in times of stress, so we turn to food. How do we know the difference? How do we know when food becomes an addiction or a problem for us? Well, one way is by asking yourself some questions.

Ask questions before you eat a food in which you know is not optimally nutritious for your body or when you feel you may be eating out of boredom or as a replacement for emotions. Some example questions are: Am I eating this anxiously? Do I desire this through my *anxious mind* or my *authentic mind*? If it's in love, joy and through the *authentic mind*, go for it, but eat slowly, close your eyes, and enjoy the savory flavor that touches your lips. Let it be a religious experience. Don't eat out of boredom, anxiety or in replacement of grief or anger. When feeling those feelings, refer to the section earlier in the book on feeling your emotions. An amazing tool I picked up from Marianne Williamson is to ask yourself, "What am I truly hungry for? What am I truly craving?" Often, we are craving peace, joy or love rather than the junk food we are preparing to binge on. Think about that before an emotional binge.

How can we incorporate fruits and veggies easily into our lives? Juicing, as I said before, is an effective, enjoyable, and easy way to make sure you get the nutrients you need. I like to make a fresh fruit salad every other day and keep it in my fridge. When you have fruits and veggies cut up and prepared, it makes it much easier to make those good choices. Cut up your favorites, throw them in a bowl and toss some cinnamon on top. It's delicious. If you don't believe these simple changes will have a big impact on your mood, try it out for yourself. Go to the grocery store and see what fresh fruits call out to you. Everyone is different, so explore what your favorites are and add in a few extra servings a day. I can promise you will quickly feel the effects.

Mindful and calm eating is also so important. Food can be a bit of a trigger for some people and practicing mindful eating is a wonderful technique to not only enjoy your food but also in watching your portions, so you don't eat until you're in pain. Try to center yourself before eating. Enjoy every bite and slow your speed down to half as fast as you normally eat. Let the utensils touch and linger on your lips. Smell every bite with your eyes closed and a soft smile on your face. Centering yourself constantly throughout the day, not just before eating, is a good way to refocus. I like to place my hand on my heart and take a deep breath to re-center. Your body is a holy and sacred space so you must ask yourself if you are treating it as such.

Movement

Our bodies want to move. They crave it. When we aren't moving our bodies regularly, they inevitably become anxious. In fact, I've actually had clients say that daily movement helps control their anxiety so much that they barely even notice it anymore. I like to use the word movement instead of exercise. The word exercise feels like a negative word to me. I feel like working out or exercise puts pressure on us to suffer or punish ourselves for the things we've eaten. Working out and exercise have become words used to describe burning calories or losing weight. There are a lot of negative body image connotations that I associate with those words, so using the word movement makes me want to actually participate in it. I used to overdo my workouts. My OCD used to run my workouts, so I would push my body to extremes. My only motivation to workout was to counteract the foods I ate so that I could keep my body weight exactly where I wanted it. Now, I understand the importance of being gentler and tuning in to what my body enjoys doing. When you decide to move your body, make sure you move it in a way that you enjoy, not in a way you dread. Moving the body should not feel like a chore. It should feel energizing, exciting, fun, joyful, and free. Don't use the movement of the body to punish the body or to counteract what you've eaten. Nourish your body, don't torture it.

Rhodiola and Other Supplements

I'm sharing what has worked for me. These supplements will absolutely not work for everyone. Unlike magnesium, these are not universally healing supplements, just ones that have helped me and others. Since I suffered from a severe magnesium deficiency for so long, magnesium was really the main supplement I was focused on; however, I did notice a difference when I began taking rhodiola rosea. I actually had my grandma and sister try this miraculous adaptogen and they both noticed a change in their anxiety and depression. I personally felt rhodiola helped my mood. I felt like my depression always lifted quite noticeably when I took it as opposed to the times when I didn't. It's definitely something worth trying because it's very safe due to its adaptogenic qualities. This means that it can help energize you when you're sluggish and adapts to your body to calm you down when your stress level raises. I always recommend taking this herb in the morning before noon. Look for one with 3% rosavin, and 1% salidroside and take 250 to 500 mg. You may notice some other benefits after taking this herb such as improved mental and physical performance. Note that if you do have a magnesium deficiency, which you most likely do if you're reading this book, it's vital to your recovery to correct that first. You can use both magnesium and rhodiola together as well if you choose to do so. Note that until you correct the magnesium, other calming herbs and supplements may not work to the best of their ability. Correcting the deficiency and trying other calming herbs later will provide you with the best results.

Ashwaganda is another powerful herb to help with anxiety. I've been using this herb for some time now and it can help not only your anxiety, but is also an anti-aging herb that helps in thyroid health as well. Sam-E has had some wonderful results helping both OCD and depression. Inositol is another great one for OCD, as well as GABA and tryptophan (5 HTP). Passion flower, california poppy, hops and valerian are great for calming, as well as lemon balm.

Try different amino acids and herbs out for yourself and see which ones work best for you. Just remember to always look at correcting deficiencies first because you don't want to use herbs as a Band-Aid to just mask a problem that can most likely be solved by correcting deficiencies.

Sleep

Sleep can be the anxiety sufferer's best friend or worst enemy. It all depends. Sleep can be scary and so stressful, even though the entire purpose of it is to be relaxing and restorative. It can make you panic and those lovely bouts of insomnia always seem to come at the worst times. This is NOT a coincidence. I'm sure you knew that already. When we are stressing so much throughout the day, we tense up our minds and bodies. It can be quite hard to shut it all down by 10 o'clock. We toss and turn and just can't seem to shut off our minds. Our bodies want and need sleep, but our *anxious minds* have a different night planned for us.

I've experienced severe bouts of insomnia. These were some of the darkest times for me. During the worst of my insomnia, I would go three days with one hour of sleep every night. It was totally horrific. I walked around like a zombie. I felt terrified of the night. It was like literally living in hell. Once I realized what I could do to help, it started to vastly improve.

The number one tool I use to help with sleep is to stop caring if I sleep or not. I know this is not the answer you expected but it's actually the most powerful tool I have found yet for insomnia. Do not dismiss the simplicity of this life-changing tool. The moment I realized I'm not going to die if I miss a few hours, I'm not going to get fired from my job, and I'm not going to accidentally ruin my health by missing a few nights of sleep, I started sleeping again. I actually would start to enjoy the hours I wasn't sleeping by doing something I liked. Seems counterproductive, but it's not. One of the worst things you can do when you can't sleep is to lie in bed for hours tossing and turning. You'll end up driving yourself completely mad and resenting the hell out of your peacefully sleeping partner (I swear I imagined murdering my husband a few of those nights just out of pure jealousy). So instead, I would get myself out of bed, go read in my living room, put a heating pad on my body (that little bit of warmth is so helpful in winding down) or even watch some TV.

I know I'm going against every piece of advice that the experts recommend for insomniacs, but I'm just sharing what has worked for me. You will be told to avoid the blue light from electronics before bed. I say this is 100% true for things like iPads, phones, and laptops but for some reason turning the TV on with low volume can actually be very soothing and just what you need to slowly doze off. I like to put on a show or movie that I enjoy but have already seen many times before. If it's a new show or film you risk forcing yourself to stay awake so not to miss an important part. Again, know your own body and what works for you.

The most common reason why people with anxiety have bouts of insomnia is because their minds are racing and bodies are tense. When it comes to sleep, people with anxiety are extremely sensitive to light, sounds and emotions. Even happy emotions can rev our bodies up so much that we can't sleep. That's OK. You'll live. Your body will sleep when it needs to. It is smarter than you think.

Another common reason why it's hard to sleep is we often subconsciously sabotage ourselves out of a good night's sleep if we know we have an exciting or important day coming up. One of the scariest things you can say to someone with anxiety the night before an important day is, "Make sure you get plenty of sleep tonight." "Oh no," is the first thing that pops into our heads. Then the thoughts begin. "What if I don't sleep well tonight? I've been looking forward to tomorrow for months now. What if I don't sleep well, I'll ruin tomorrow. I won't enjoy it!" These are all totally and completely normal thought processes and don't fret about it if you experience them. In fact, I've had many events where I barely slept the night before but they were still some of the best days of my life. My wedding is still the best memory and best day of my life that I've ever had. I lived in every moment and slept no more than a half an hour the night before. On the morning of my wedding day, I remember waking up panicked. "Oh no," I thought. "I only slept thirty minutes last night! This is the day I've waited for my entire life. I'm going to ruin it. I'm going to have bags under my eyes…" The thoughts of my *anxious mind* went on and on. You get the idea.

Of course, in the morning, I felt it too. Physically, I felt disoriented and panicked. My *anxious mind* latched onto those limiting thoughts I had been feeding it all morning long. I felt exhausted and like I couldn't move. That's how powerful the mind is. It can make you feel so sick and tired. I decided to stop and breathe. I slowed down and started to make a choice to choose *authentic mind*. I did a meditation and a prayer to try and calm myself down so I could enjoy the day. At first, my body felt better, but still not great. In that moment, I just decided to accept it. I told myself everything, absolutely everything happens for a reason. If this is how I'm supposed to feel on my wedding day, then I'm going to enjoy it. Enjoy the tiredness, the disorientation and the dizziness. I was accepting the things I couldn't change and making it a joyous day, even if I felt horrible.

Then, a funny thing happened. It just went away. When I released my expectations, quieted my mind, and accepted the things I had no power over, I felt massively better. I got out of the way and stopped trying to control. I kind of gave up for a minute, shrugged my shoulders, and told myself "it is what it is." Sometimes giving up and throwing your hands in the air out of frustration and defeat is the exact thing you need to do. The moment you drop that controlling, manic, strung-out feeling and go with the flow for just a minute is when real change occurs. After that, my friends and family started piling into my hotel room. Everyone was so excited and running around trying to get ready. I stopped, took a step back, and looked at all of them, realizing how truly lucky I was. Then I allowed myself to get excited and all my physical symptoms vanished.

It's also important to take daily action towards calming the body. Doing so will automatically calm the mind. It's so important in panic and anxiety prevention because it allows us not to even get put in those difficult situations in the first place, like I was on my wedding day. When I got married, I was strung out all the time. I did not relax my body or mind on a daily basis. I only relaxed and meditated when I felt incredibly stressed, which always was too late. Putting relaxation into your daily routine conditions both the mind and body for rest. When you slow down the breath, you automatically slow down the mind. When the body begins to relax, the mind follows. We need to take the pressure off of sleep and stop obsessing about every hour we get or don't get. We need to set aside the sleep tracking devices and chill. Go to bed late sometimes and break the rules. It's OK.

Another good tip is to take time to unwind before bed. Perhaps you want to put some essential oils on your body to calm yourself, do some calming stretches, or meditate before bed. Don't go to bed stressed out at 10 pm because you have to wake up at 5 am. Wait until 11:00 pm, midnight, or 12:30 am before you crawl into bed if that's how long it takes to bring your body down. I will never go to bed stressed, worried, or wired anymore. That means going to bed at 2:00 am some nights, and I'm good with that. I would rather get six hours than no hours of sleep. Tossing and turning kills your sleep. Take the pressure off and you will start sleeping better eventually. Be patient. Your body will regulate itself. The key to good sleep is to relax throughout the entire day, so the body isn't expected to quickly calm down as soon as your head hits the pillow. That's just an unrealistic expectation of your body. You're not going to get much sleep if that is how your life is structured. Make some changes, relax throughout your entire day, take the pressure off, and you'll be sleeping better before you know it.

Meditation

For a long time, I couldn't figure out what the purpose of meditation was. I knew it was a way in which to relax, but I never really considered it to be an essential part of my life. I wondered how much it could actually do. It seemed a bit too "out there" for me. I feared that people were going to think I was stupid for doing it. I didn't know how I was going to be able to shut off my mind.

So, with that said, my first meditation attempts went something like this...

"Am I thinking? I'm not supposed to be thinking. Clear your mind. OK, I see clouds. Let the thoughts pass like a cloud. Okay, I see a dog in the cloud, I don't really like dogs. I remember that time the dog licked my leg and I had to go inside and wash my leg. That was so gross. I wonder if that dog downstairs is going to bark again today. OMG stop thinking Tosha! OMG, this isn't working, screw it, I want some pie!" No wonder I wasn't into meditation after experiences like these. So, I decided to wash my hands of it. I figured it clearly wasn't for me. I was putting so much pressure on myself to actually calm down and breathe that I wasn't doing either. I was getting more stressed because I couldn't master meditation. For a year, I stopped meditating.

In spite of my perceived failure, something still told me that I needed this time of stillness. So, I attempted meditation again. I still couldn't seem to really connect with a specific meditation. The more I looked at different types of mantras and certain breathing techniques, the more I realized I needed something way simpler for my mind to start as a beginner. So, I had a little epiphany. I realized that for me, all I had to do was sit still. I didn't even call it meditating for some time because the whole word seemed to intimidate me and make me feel as though I wasn't doing it right.

I began having daily stillness time. I put it into my routine every single day. By just simply sitting still, I was able to curb my craving for calm. The beautiful thing about this discovery was the more I learned to sit still and breathe for just five, ten, then fifteen minutes, my mind automatically calmed down without me even having to focus on it. The mind actually does automatically calm down when you sit still and close your eyes. When your body is still, your mind will soon follow, without you having to obsess about the "how." In fact, the "how" is not important. Your body is smart. It calms your mind for you.

I also started to notice that many answers to questions and worries that I was having came easier to me when I just sat still and took some breaths. A quote by Yogi Bhajan reads, "Prayer is talking to God. Meditation is letting God talk to you." I realized that I could pray all I wanted, but I had to actually sit still, breathe, and calm down to get my answers. If you're trying to make choices, it's important to have an intention set before you meditate. Daily stillness and silence will decide your good choices for you. Taking time to be consciously still every single day will change your life. Being still, closing your eyes, focusing on your breath and clearing your mind will allow you to make the best choices.

Studies have shown that meditating twice a day can truly help your sleep cycle too. I know people who have even gone into recovery from severe addictions after adopting a daily meditation practice. We must attempt to silence the constant internal chatter we experience daily. Meditation is an excellent way of doing so. Simply sitting still and focusing on your breath for as little as five minutes every day has shown to have benefits. I'm not talking small benefits here either. I'm talking about eating habits, health, and better relationships. It's also vital to check in with your body at least once a day to notice any tension and release it. That subtle tension every day can build up to some serious problems with your health down the road.

The more I started slowing my body, breath, mind, and life down, the more I could hear my intuition. See, we kind of lose ourselves, especially with the busyness of *anxious thoughts* whirling around in our minds. Anxiety and mental illnesses make it that much harder for us to tune into our gut feelings. We are overly distracted. Everything is too loud so we need to quiet our lives, and slow down. The answer is to force that calm into your daily life. If you are desperately seeking peace, sleep, and calm, meditation is a huge piece of the puzzle that has most likely been missing. If you feel like no matter what you do, it's just not working, be still and see what comes of it. I can promise you that curbing your daily calm craving will change your life. Commit to ten minutes a day for thirty days. Make it one of your new daily habits and you won't regret it. I promise you won't regret it.

Chapter 14
Addiction and Anxiety

When we abuse our bodies through addictions, we send our bodies and minds the message that we are not worthy of health and love. Addictions are a replacement for feeling all the intense feelings that anxiety and depression can bring. A way to numb ourselves, if you will. Addictions are a way of self-inflicting harm onto our bodies, and trust me, I've lived through my fair share of addictions. I have smoked, drank, been unable to sleep without pills, had an eating disorder, and used drugs to numb me from my pain. There is a very important difference between enjoying a drink and having an addiction problem. You can have an addiction problem if you're only using these substances once and awhile or daily. Frequency doesn't mean much to me when I define an addiction. It's all about the mindset in which you have when reaching for that drink. Are you drinking the wine or beer to avoid feeling your feelings? Or are you just enjoying the taste and the social time with friends? There is a huge difference. If you can't unwind without a substance, that's also a pretty clear sign that an addiction may be present. If you get irate when you don't have your substance, that is another sign. If you use substances when you're mad, hurt, sad or in pain, that's also a pretty good indication.

The reasons as to why people with anxiety have addiction issues comes down to a few things, one of which we talked about above and that's an avoidance of feelings. Instead of feeling our feelings, we numb them with substances. Trauma is one of the top reasons for addictions, because trauma can be so difficult to navigate and deal with, especially childhood trauma. Instead of releasing our pain and emotional wounds of our past, we hold them in and get more *anxious* and addicted.

Another reason is some adults also have no clue how to enjoy themselves without substances. In a way, these substances help adults to return to their childlike states and true, *authentic selves*. Think about it, how often do you see a group of guys hugging and telling one another how much they love each other when they're drunk? We all do and say things when we are under the influence we would never say or do otherwise. This is because our souls have been blocked from emotions. We are always so nervous about rejection or what others will think, that we don't express our emotions freely enough when we are sober.

Another reason people with anxiety and mental illness turn to substances is to loosen up. It's more challenging for us to enjoy life and have fun due to "The Tripod of Anxiety," so substances seem like the answer. We need to learn and teach ourselves how to experience *authentic* joy and genuine excitement when we are sober and to express our emotions more freely on a regular basis. That way our emotions don't become blocked up inside of us, just dying to get out. It takes practice, but it's attainable and realistic.

When I began to smoke, I was about 19 years old. I used smoking as an anti-anxiety tool after I had several traumatic events happen in my life, most notably, when my grandfather died. He was the best person I've ever known and when he died, my world totally shattered. In order to deal with the grief, OCD convinced me to pick up the addiction of smoking. I felt as if I had to physically harm my body to avoid feeling the intense grief. Fast forward to when I decided to quit and smoking became a part of my identity. It was my "screw you" to the world, my vice, and my way of dealing with any anger or stress. Cigarettes became my safety. I decided to quit after realizing the cigarette no longer provided for me what I once thought it did. In fact, instead of calming me down, it was actually making my anxiety worse. That's how addiction works. At the beginning, you feel elated and like it's the solution to all of your problems, when actually it's a way in which to avoid absolutely everything you shouldn't be avoiding. If you want success in your life and in your anxiety, the addictions have to go. Not right away, but you have to be open to them leaving. When I set out to quit, I couldn't imagine enjoying life without my cigarettes. It's funny how life works. Ten years before I started smoking, I could never have imagined myself as a smoker and after ten years into it, I couldn't imagine my life without it. That's the beauty of life. Things can change, and we have the power to change them.

After smoking for about ten years, I decided to quit. My first attempt didn't go so well. I stopped for about five days and then I went away for the weekend. Vacations were always a time when I smoked a bit more, but this time, I had so much pressure on myself to make sure that I didn't smoke. I kind of set myself up for failure. I had huge expectations for myself and about ten minutes into the trip, I couldn't function. I was sitting in a parking lot with a cigarette in my hand within the first hour. I felt so down and like a total failure. I went five whole days without one, and I couldn't believe what I had done. How could I not go one hour without a smoke? I quickly emailed my personal coach in a panic and told her that I had failed. She emailed me back and explained I had put too many expectations on myself. She assured me that I would quit when the time was right and I shouldn't try so hard to force things. That feeling of failure slowly began to lift. I realized it was only temporary.

I decided to forgive myself and kept smoking the rest of the weekend without any pressure. I told myself I could smoke whenever I wanted to and that Monday, I would quit and never smoke again. I took the pressure off, learned from it, set myself up for success, and moved on. The next trip I took, I didn't even crave a cigarette. In fact, it was one of the best trips I ever had. I changed my focus from the cigarette onto other, more enjoyable things. I rediscovered my *authentic self* on that second trip.

I have found something interesting about addictions. Most people with anxiety and mental illness don't know how to really take care and nurture themselves. Maybe they do when they're sick, but they don't really self-care or nurture themselves until there is a reason to. If you're sick, that's a justifiable reason. Addictions are a way to make ourselves sick so we can take care of ourselves. We drink until we are so hungover the next day, and part of the reason is the mind's subconscious need for self-care. To re-coup and take care of ourselves on that hangover day. I remember that as much as I hated the feeling of being sick, I subconsciously liked being forced to slow down. I would run myself a bath and whine a bit on the couch while my husband made me tea and put cozy blankets on me. I liked taking care of myself, so I felt justified to rest.

I always felt as though no one ever really noticed how much I suffered inside of my head 24/7. A part of me liked being sick so I could feel that extra understanding and kindness from others. Most of all, I gave myself a break when I was sick. I was always so obsessively hard on myself and I knew I could rest and escape the pressure when I was sick. It's almost a way for addicts to nourish themselves. We make ourselves sick (hungover) so that we can recoup, take care of ourselves, eat the food we want, rest, and nurture ourselves guilt-free. We don't feel like we have to go to the gym or work. It's a way to kind of force the body to self-care. Sickness = safety. This is so true for hangovers. I mean, how many times have you had a drink with someone who says, "This is going to hurt tomorrow." Sometimes, we take part in these behaviors so it forces us to self-care. The solution to this is daily self-care. If you feel like you can relate to this, the answer is to properly and healthily take care of yourself. You are worth that.

Wouldn't it be amazing if we could just do that for ourselves daily so we don't have that human need unfulfilled? What if we didn't need to turn to our addictions to provide us with *authentic* joy and genuine nurturing? Well, we can. We can learn and practice tuning into our *authentic minds* daily. The more we turn from *anxious mind* to *authentic mind*, the more easily the addictions will start to diminish. We will actually become more averse to them and no longer feel the need to have them in our lives. They will no longer serve a purpose to us.

You will gently notice negative things in your life begin to fall away and the things of joy and love will start to slowly seep in. This way, you can enjoy the process of healing. You will know the right time to drop the negative things that no longer serve you. Putting pressure on yourself and totally quitting things cold turkey while you "white knuckle" your entire day minute by minute is not ideal for people with anxiety. A gentle method is more approachable and the results are life-long.

Here are some great tips to help if you're trying to quit smoking or other addictive patterns:

- Take things in small steps like try changing a pattern for one or two days; try half a day or one day without cigarettes

- Switch up your addiction's routine. If you're used to having a pill or cigarette when you first wake up, have one 30 minutes later. If you have three drinks before bed, have a drink one night and three again the following night. These routines keep you stuck, so change them and be creative. The more these routines change, the more your mind has difficulty keeping track. It's good to confuse your *anxious mind*.

- Try staring at the substance you feel you abuse and journal about why you feel like you need it.

- Journal about when you started the addiction and see if you can make connections to situational things or your anxiety severity at that time (often there are connections here such as I began smoking when my grandpa died).

- Don't put time pressure on yourself, and give yourself a mental "out." I actually quit smoking by taking it day by day and telling myself that if I really wanted one, I could have one. I took it moment by moment and before I knew it, months had passed by.

- Write in your journal what you look forward to doing/feeling when you quit your addiction.

- While you quit, journal daily about the new-found time and benefits you've gained by quitting.

- Enjoy the quitting process. Choose to enjoy it through *authentic thoughts* and not *anxious* ones. Remember, a majority of withdrawal symptoms are in our minds disguised as truth from the *anxious mind*.

- When you have a craving, go outside and take in some fresh air, and write a gratitude list.

- Replace your addiction with some fresh green juice with fruit. It actually tastes great. It will give you the nutritional boost you need to fight the craving, as well as keep you motivated and loving your new healthy body.

- Workout

- Meditate or try alternate nostril breath to calm you.

- Use "The Five Senses of Peace" often

- Ask yourself "What am I actually craving?" The answer is probably peace. Remember your addictions can't feed the need for peace.

- Wean off substances slowly.

Physical withdrawals are always made worse by our anxiety and fear of living without the substance than it actually is the substance withdrawal itself. That's one thing people don't often look at. Anytime I was focused on missing my cigarettes, the physical withdrawal symptoms were worse than when I became grateful for my addiction-free life. When you become excited and grateful for all of the benefits you will gain from abandoning your addictions (which honestly are endless), your quitting process becomes much more manageable and enjoyable. I learned this from Alan Carr's book, "The Easy Way to Stop Smoking."

Quit things peacefully, not forcefully. The time will come when you can look at a cigarette or bottle of alcohol and say thank you for serving your purpose in my life, but I no longer need you anymore. Remember, you are now a new person. You know new information that you can't unlearn. You are ready to release these negative things and trust me, it can be a lot easier than you ever thought possible. Quit in joy. Get excited for how your body will feel. Do something fun with the money you'll save. Get pumped to release the self-loathing and guilt that accompanies addictions. You will know when you're ready. Just keep going at it, because with every small step towards *the authentic mind*, your addictions get weaker and weaker.

Section Three
"Break a Leg": Outlook and Mindset

As I spoke about earlier, each section in this book is created to weaken each leg of "The Tripod of Anxiety." One by one we will help dismantle each leg. The following section focuses on outlook and mindset.

Chapter 15
Self-Love

Self-love has a strange reputation. There are a lot of misconceptions around the phrase "self-love." It seemed like a hoax to me when I was first introduced to it. I now realize that was because I knew I didn't have any to give myself. Like most of the things we need desperately in our lives, it's easier to be skeptical of them than to try and fail at them. It was a way for me to deny my own self-love. I associated it with being too selfish or arrogant for me. I now realize what a massively underplayed issue it is and how much it needs to be addressed. A lot of daily conflicts we encounter can be traced back to our lack of self-love. How do you think people end up bitter, abusing themselves, stay in bad relationships, or make poor choices? Almost every one of those situations can be traced back to a lack of self-love.

I didn't love myself. I never had. I had no clue what it even meant. That's a really clear sign right there. If you don't understand what self-love means, you are probably in desperate need of it because when you finally have that love for yourself, you can clearly define what it is. When I had none, it constantly showed in my actions. I had addictions, would feel like I wanted revenge on people who had hurt me, ate poorly, slept poorly, said "yes" to things I never wanted to do, and was a huge people pleaser. We can waste a lot of time not loving ourselves and dismiss it as not being important, but deep down we instinctively know if we unconditionally love ourselves or not. Again, if you aren't sure, chances are that you could use some self-love.

A lack of self-love is not a badge of honor. In fact, you are not only hurting yourself with this problem, you are hurting your children, your husband, your wife, your parents, and your friends. You aren't doing anyone any favors by not loving yourself. In fact, you are teaching all the people around you not to love themselves either while believing that lacking self-love makes you a less selfish, more compassionate person. A lack of self-love truly extends into every single area of your life. You don't always know it is behind certain actions that you do.

People suffering from mental illness and anxiety already have a lot of guilt for their conditions. Guilt is like a breeding ground for self-loathing. I always felt guilty for my OCD. I also blamed myself for my mother's panic attacks and anxiety, and I told myself it was because of my OCD. I felt guilt for missing out on social engagements and that I was a burden to everyone around me. I felt guilty for feeling. I ruined family holidays because I would need everything a certain way in order to feel comfortable and it was noticed. I felt the most guilt for my times of depression.

This guilt is where my lack of self-love began. I learned self-loathing from nearly every member of my family. I did not have many examples of self-love around me and I just thought that was normal. As I began journaling, coaching, and releasing my emotions using tools such as tapping, I was able to release my guilt. This opened a door for me to truly learn the connection between self-love and recovery from mental illness.

You can't heal if you don't learn how to love yourself unconditionally first. You now have the chance to give yourself the love you have always wanted and deserve. Self-love is something you need to work on and, like everything else in this book, you need to practice and commit to it.

It's important to note that if we are constantly giving love to others without giving it to ourselves, we end up feeling resentful and drained. We absolutely must fill ourselves up with total and complete love first so that our minds and bodies are overflowing with it. When something overflows, it means we possess that very thing in abundance and have plenty to share with others. We must look at love that way too. If we aren't overflowing with love but still giving love and support freely to others, we are giving to them from an empty vessel. That's how we get tired and sick. We continually keep giving others what we simply do not have. We become bankrupt in love.

Journal Break:

In our deepest and darkest times of anxiety and depression, we can feel like we don't have love from others. I can tell you this for sure, we all have more love than we think we have. I challenge you to make a love list. Really look at the people in your life that make you feel loved. Take some time and really think about people in your past and present. I don't care if they're easily accessible or if they live halfway across the world. I want you to write them on this list. Just the simple task of writing it down, reflecting, and having this list available to you is more therapeutic than you may think. What do they do to make you feel that way? How can you do these things for yourself?

The following are a few of my favorite unconventional ways to show self-love:

The Art of Not Caring What Others Think

This is one of my favorite self-love tools and it is one of the best acts of self-love we can do. Most of us care what other people think too much. This is part of our *anxious minds'* programming. We are extremely conscious of others' thoughts and opinions of us. We would be incredibly hesitant to dress up in a funny costume on a day other than Halloween and sit in a restaurant. It would take a lot of convincing and dares for us to do something like that. This is just the way society has been conditioned. So why do we care so much about others' opinions of us? We even care about what strangers think of us. It's because of our programming. We try hard to make good first impressions, especially with people like potential bosses or in-laws. We want people to like us and may even lie when people ask us our opinions on something, if we think it's what they want to hear.

Why is it so important that others approve and like us? Well, so often these types of patterns have been passed down through generations. People pleasers usually come from a long line of people pleasers, and it can be one of the unhealthiest traits to have. Fortunately, this is all attributed to conditioning. Just like we have been so conditioned to think a certain way, we can condition ourselves to change our minds and make that our new story. People pleasing can also be a result of trauma. Whatever the reason is behind your desire for needing people to like you or your extreme consciousness of what others think, you can change.

It would be a shocking revelation to see how many choices we make based on our fear of what others will think of us. The fact of the matter is it doesn't matter at all. In the big picture, we will screw up. The people that are worth it will forgive us, and the people who aren't may leave us. We have so many reasons as to why people come into our lives and sometimes it's just more important for them to leave than it is for them to stay. Some people are meant to be involved with us for a short time and then are supposed to leave. These situations are only as bad as we make them. It's more important that we honor and respect ourselves, love who we are, and keep promises to ourselves. We only have to worry about whether or not we are good people doing what we can do to be kind and loving. As long as our intentions are for the greater good, we have nothing else to be concerned about. Everyone will mess up because we are human. There is no point wasting your time on the people who are going to judge the hell out of you anyways.

A good tip for getting past this roadblock is to set an intention for one week to challenge your thoughts. Challenge the thoughts you have around worrying about others' opinions of you. Grab your journal and after each day, track some scenarios where you hesitated to speak or acted out of fear of what others' think. This can also be described as playing small when you should be going big. Maybe you weren't honest about how you felt or maybe you obsessed about what you said or did. This can be an eye-opening exercise. The first time I tried this, I realized that I hesitated to post certain things on social media, afraid I would offend someone. I noticed how often I questioned myself after I sent a text message. I worried about how I looked when I ran into someone I knew. So be aware and open your eyes to it. You will be surprised how often you make choices based on this fear.

Forgiveness

Forgiveness is challenging, but it's also one of the best things we can do. We must forgive others, as well as ourselves, if we ever desire a better life. Forgiveness is not something you can fake. You can't trick yourself into forgiving. You can't say that you forgive people and then bring up those same past hurts a day or two later. You either forgive, or you haven't been able to yet, and that's OK. True and complete forgiveness is probably one of the hardest things to do.

First of all, we need to understand we all mess up. Not one of us has gone through life unscathed in this area. We are flawed beings and that's actually a good thing. It's what makes life interesting. Secondly, we need to understand everyone is trying and doing the very best they can with the information they have. Think about it. Are you doing the best you can do with the information you have right now? Of course you are. Are there things you will do today that you'll look back in three years from now and you wish you hadn't done? Of course. We are all learning and expanding our knowledge daily. We won't be the same people in three years that we are today. We are all doing the best we can do with the knowledge and understanding we have. Three years ago, I was a much more bitter person than I am today. I've learned so much about my own struggles with anxiety and how holding grudges from past hurts only hurt me. We are all at different levels of our healing journey; therefore, we must remember not to judge. We each have a specific and individualized journey and need to learn specific life lessons from them.

No two people have experienced the same event in the same way. It's all about perspective and our life experiences. The mind is an incredibly complex thing, so we need to learn how to give one another a break. We don't think exactly the same way. This is the case even if you've grown up together in the same family and in the same house. One child may develop into an adult who is a workaholic, while the other is an alcoholic. Which one do you think society accepts and celebrates more? You see, we all interpret events and experiences differently. Be kind and be patient with people. Just because you think something should be done a certain way does not make it the right way. You need to understand this to move forward in your recovery from anxiety. Our *anxious mind* thrives on anger, judgement, grudges and unforgiveness.

We must learn how to be quick to forgive and slow to anger. Repeat that - quick to forgive and slow to anger. This is a message we all need to be reminded of daily, sometimes even hourly. Why is forgiving others so essential to our recovery? It's so important because unresolved anger and grudges are two of the top emotions that cause anxiety. These emotions can subconsciously boil under the surface and then manifest in our actions. You may not even know you're experiencing these emotions, but I can guarantee you've probably got some forgiving to do.

How do we forgive? Well, forgiveness is actually a lifelong and daily process. You will not go through the rest of your life without getting hurt by another human being. It just won't happen. We have opportunities to forgive others quickly as well as forgiving ourselves daily. These opportunities are always there for us. Perhaps someone cuts you off driving on the highway or your spouse does something that makes you feel unheard and uncared for. These are common daily challenges that are opportunities to practice your new forgiveness tool.

Now, for the deep dark hurts of your past. The ones where you feel betrayed or maybe even hatred. Perhaps you've been through a trauma and now need to forgive someone you feel doesn't deserve your forgiveness. There are definitely situations where others may not deserve your forgiveness, but you deserve it. You deserve to be set free from the damaging shame, fear, pain, and disdain you feel deep inside of your soul. You deserve to be free from the toll these emotions have taken on your life, body and health. You deserve the joyful moments you missed while you were being controlled by this darkness. These hurts and pains will take much more time to move past than others. These hurts and pains may need a professional to support you in your times of healing and forgiveness.

If you desire to have that freedom, your healing and ability to forgive and move on will come, but it may take time. You may need to do forgiveness exercises daily with this particular person and situation in mind. You may need to write a letter to this person that you will never send, or write in your journal every day. You may need to do tapping daily with forgiveness in your heart. These wounds take time to heal. Forgive everyday until you feel it release. No expert can tell you how long that will take. You are the expert and you will feel it when you're ready to move on. It's a beautiful experience.

Forgiving ourselves is just as important as forgiving others. As I mentioned earlier, we often feel a lot of guilt for our anxiety problems. I carried my guilt for a long time without even realizing it. I always thought I was abnormal and spoke down to myself. Just because we are different than other people does not make us abnormal. Remember, there are many positive and beautiful traits that anxiety sufferers possess. These traits make the world a better place. This is just a kind reminder that I want you to remember in your heart. You are as normal as anyone else. Maybe you have felt strange for your anxiety or maybe other people made you feel like you're weird when you were a child, teenager, or even as an adult. Well, you're not weird. We are all unique individuals. Who creates the standards of what is normal? We are all normal and we are all abnormal at the same time. We must forgive these thoughts we have about ourselves and others in order to have unconditional self-love.

Journal Break:

I want you to reflect on love. How do you view love? Is love unconditional? What have your experiences with love been in the past? Record this in your journal. How do you express love to others? Is it conditional or unconditional?

Sometimes we can love others unconditionally and not feel worthy of that same love ourselves.

Stop Comparing Yourself to Others

Don't compare yourself to other people. Be happy for others when they succeed and don't make other people's successes your failures. They are your successes too. All these successes do is simply show you what you are capable of. Other people's successes, in anxiety recovery and in all areas of life, should just be used as inspiration to see what your potential is. We live in a highly judgmental and comparative society, where success and failure can be measured by comparing ourselves to others. Social media is the perfect example of this. We are constantly scrolling through our pages looking at the beautiful pictures and travels of our friends and our lives start to feel lacking. We were programmed to compare from childhood. Comparison occurs in school, sports, family, and even friendships. At a young age, we can start to feel disappointed and a little deflated about ourselves by comparing our accomplishments with others who may have done better than us. Does this diminish the amazingness of your accomplishment? Absolutely not, yet somehow we feel like it does. We are no longer the best, and it hits us hard. Others' success should be nothing but motivation.

Chapter 16
Embracing Your Immaturity

When we were kids, we thought that growing up meant more freedom. More freedom equals more happiness, yet when we become adults, we generally become unhappier and dissatisfied with our lives. We are constantly telling stories from our youth about all the amazing times we had, the trouble we got into, the rules we bent, and all the people we mooned. Yup, you read that correctly. I said mooned. So, when we were kids, we wanted to be adults and now that we are adults, we want to be kids. We see that we live our entire lives wanting to be in a different stage than we actually are in. We live in the past or future most of the time and rarely live in the moment.

Living in the moment is not easy for anyone. Those with anxiety are constantly worrying about the future and fixating on mistakes of the past. We need to practice and prioritize things like living in the moment, embracing our immaturity, and letting down our walls. We must practice it. We don't spend a lot of time actually working on our joy or living in the moment.

Wouldn't it be so cool to go back and experience life as a baby or a young child, untarnished by life's difficulties? Wouldn't it be cool to know what we know now and go back and experience life in a totally different way? Wouldn't we appreciate it so much more? Well, believe it or not, you can decide today to have a new story and a new life. You can give yourself the childhood you never had, now! You can use your childhood interests and passions as a means to explore your life today. What did you enjoy doing as a child?

Journal Break

I want you to stop here, pull out your journal and write about your childhood dreams and desires. What were your beliefs about the world when you were a child? How have they changed?

So, how does connecting to your childlike self and embracing your immaturity assist in your anxiety recovery? Well, when we were children, we were closest to our true selves or *authentic minds*. We rarely leaned towards the *anxious mind* unless we were taught to - unless we observed the adults or other children around us doing so. Naturally, we leaned towards our *authentic minds* and peace. The world around us makes it difficult now to be our *authentic* selves. We walk around in a total *anxious mind* bubble without even being aware of it.

As the years passed, we disconnected from that *authentic mind*. We have had positive experiences, but since the *anxious mind* is fed more than the *authentic*, the negative experiences are the ones that stand out. They have been tattooed into our minds on a subconscious level. We feed the *anxious mind* as adults and that *anxious mind* holds onto those traumatic and negative life experiences more easily than the positive ones.

What's the solution? We have to keep life fun. We have to set time aside to have fun. We need to be silly and childlike. Go bowling, go to an arcade, or go to the movies. When I need some fun, I ride on a roller coaster. That is pure fun to me. What images in your mind stick out when you think of the word "fun?" We have to take time to savor the pleasures in life. You can never do that enough. You can't overdo joy or take too much time enjoying life. It is something we don't do enough, but it is also the entire point of living. We were not meant to be stuck looking at the same four walls our entire lives. We were meant to explore, evolve, grow, and enjoy the world.

We tend to get so busy, moody and impatient that we don't often take the time to enjoy things as simple as our food - eating slowly, smelling the food, and savoring the tastes. We don't stop to watch the falling snow at night or the beautiful Christmas lights. Pleasure means different things to different people. Take some time to appreciate everything in your life and be delighted in it. Take time to relish and revel in gratitude. Be overjoyed for the family members and friends all around you who are alive and well. There is never ever a time when it is too late to enjoy your life. A common regret people have as they age is that they didn't appreciate or enjoy the little things enough. They spent too much time cleaning their houses and worrying about bills. Don't let these regrets be yours.

Some ways in which we can reconnect to this part of ourselves are:

Do something that inspires you.

When you are inspired, you are "in spirit." Being inspired for me means talking to my husband about our future dreams. I love talking to a safe person about my future and about all the dreams

I have. You can also sit down and write these things out. Get excited and inspired about possibilities. Hold back nothing. Other ways to become inspired is to create. You may enjoy painting, singing, rapping or writing. Create something! It's a fun way to get inspired.

Go to your favorite place.

I know when I feel sapped and exhausted, that's when I know I need to go to my favorite place, which is Niagara Falls. Any person who truly knows me knows that I adore this place. It makes me feel happy and free and helps me to truly embrace my immaturity. Your place may be a destination, a coffee shop, a shopping mall, anything. Don't judge your happiness place and don't let others judge it either. If you are being drawn towards a certain place or a feeling of really wanting to go somewhere or do something, just do it. Screw what everyone else has to say about it.

Be a little irresponsible.

Life's too short to be responsible 24/7. Sneak into a hotel swimming pool, take some risks, jump out of a plane, crash a wedding or party and make up fake names. Just get out there and be a little irresponsible. Don't break the law, but bend the rules on occasion. Let loose a bit and lighten up.

Some other things I love to do:
- **Build a fort out of couch cushions**
- **Have a party**

- **Get creative**

- **Have an Easter egg hunt**

- **Go on the swings (swings are THE best!)**

- **Jump on a giant trampoline**

- **Prank call my friends (When did prank calling stop becoming a thing?)**

Why do you think people latch on so much to nostalgic things from their past? It's not the pictures, toys, or bands they care so much about, it's more about the memories attached to them. Going to see a band you listened to as a teenager reminds you of the amazing times spent with friends. A simpler time free from technology and full of laughter. We can get those times back by connecting with people and having fun.

When we were kids, my cousins and I would go underwater for hours in the pool outside. We would scream, put goggles on, and make funny faces at each other. At night, we loved to swim. It was magical and beautiful. Why is it that as kids, we can spend hours underwater making funny faces at one another, but as adults, we cannot? No drinking, no drugs, no cell phones and no artificial stimulation. It's boring. So, why is this so boring to us? As adults, we claim to have more focus and concentration than children do, yet the thought of doing something like that for an hour just seems boring. We've lost our wonder and imagination. We forget how healing these activities were for us. We must remember that we can get back to a place where we swim for an hour and laugh hysterically with our friends. We just have to practice finding our joy. The more we practice this, the easier and more genuine those moments become. We have to remove those blocks and limiting beliefs we have around maturity and the fact that we genuinely believe that excitement is only reserved for ages 2 to 14.

We are open and trusting when we are younger, but we must understand that our childhood was not the only time that we can be happy. As we get older, it may not come as naturally to us. We have to make an effort to re-discover our joy. Doesn't that sound fun? Trust me, the more we tap into that, the more loving and peaceful of a world we will live in. So go stick your finger in the bowl and eat the icing, jump on the trampoline, and laugh like you've never laughed before.

Journal Break

Who were you as a child? What were your interests? Things that you never do now? The stuff you loved doing as a kid, you did for a reason. If you loved playing guitar, you loved it because that is who you really are. If you loved dancing and singing, that was you being your authentic self, with your walls down. You loved these things for a reason. We put walls up and then forget what our true interests are. Your true selves and personalities were exposed as children. Your true talents and interests that made you unique are you. We need to go find that person again!

Become Curious

Curiosity is key in the recovery process. I learned a lot about the importance of curiosity when I quit smoking. Allow me to explain. Smoking had become part of my identity. When I would go away in the summer with my husband and we would sneak away to our favorite place, cigarettes would be a big part of that. I used them to help calm me down and get me into "vacation mode." They were a way for me to relax after a nice swim or I'd have one after eating ice cream. Basically, anytime I felt stressed, relaxed, bored or hungry, I'd grab one. I talked about my experience with quitting earlier in this book, but what I didn't talk about was what I discovered when I finally did it successfully.

When I successfully quit, I took the opportunities that I would normally be having a cigarette, to reconnect with my childlike, *authentic* self. I laughed, I climbed trees, and I became curious about the world around me. I slowed down and began to notice things more. At the beginning, I actually had to force myself to slow down and notice things. Cigarettes always amped me up, so I figured I'd use the opportunities during my quitting process to slow down. I would feel the pleasures of life around me more without that cigarette distracting me. I was rediscovering myself. This addiction I had, distracted me for over ten years because I was always focused on when my next cigarette would be. I missed out on a lot of beauty around me and some fun too. Since quitting, I have totally rediscovered myself. I've reconnected with childlike interests and reignited my sense of wonder in the world. I realized I don't need to have all the answers to be successful. In fact, understanding that I didn't have all the answers at all was empowering. As adults, we think we know so much and have got the world figured out, but we don't. It's more freeing to admit that we don't have all the answers as opposed to trying to control everything around us and thinking we're smarter than everyone else.

I really want you to take this chapter seriously. Becoming our *authentic* selves is so important for true happiness. In general, we live in a fearful place. We obsessively worry and spend so much wasted time thinking about ridiculous things that will not matter to us in ten years. Embracing your immaturity or childlike, *authentic self* actually gives you a new perspective on life. It helps you to become more and do more. We need more smiles, more laughter, and more fun in our lives. Let the small stuff go. Let the weeds in the backyard grow a bit, and don't worry about the stains on your clothes. The world won't fall apart if you decide to leave work early to go on a roller coaster.

Chapter 17
Faith and Anxiety

Have you ever seen the movie, "The Santa Clause" with Tim Allen? It's a 90's classic. I love that movie. It's the perfect Christmas movie, and like most Christmas movies, it deals with the theme around believing in things that are not reasonable or logical. If you remember in this movie, the boy's stepdad is an uptight therapist who is successful, practical and unbelieving of anything that doesn't make scientific sense to him, aka the regular, educated, modern grown-up. Tim Allen's character essentially turns into Santa Claus because the original Santa fell off of Allen's roof. I believe it was Shakespeare that came up with that plot line. At the end, everyone, even the uptight adults, let down their walls and finally begin to believe in miracles again.

See, as kids we believe in everything, and then we grow up. We grow out of belief, wonder and excitement. We like to think we have everything figured out. We take the wonder out of life and only listen to practical stuff. We stop believing in things like Santa Claus, miracles, and just about anything we can't understand or explain, even God. At some point in our childhood, we found out the truth about Santa and our little hearts were shattered. But, we moved on, pretty emotionally undamaged, or at least that's what we thought. Not believing in things like Santa was just the beginning of our cynicism about things like God, love, and miracles.

The concept of Santa seems just way too wonderful and magical, so our cynical minds figure it must not be true. That's not real. That's not life. The sooner our kids realize that, the better. Life is not magical, it's practical. Except, we missed the truth that it is magical. It can actually be even more than magical. It can be miraculous!

If we could all pray to see the world through a child's eyes, life would look very different. As I've said before, it was when we were children that we were closest to being our true, *authentic* selves. When we become like children, our walls go down and we can love and trust unconditionally in such a natural way. The world around us becomes magical. What we don't know is that seeing the world through the eyes of a child, with all its beauty, is possible for adults too. When we tear down those walls we've put up and just practice loving people, trusting and believing, the most miraculous things start to unfold in our lives.

Have you ever looked at a child and thought, "Ugh, I remember being that happy! I wish I could go back in time, be a kid, and see the world through the eyes of a child?"

Often, we want those feelings back. Little do we know, those feelings and answers are inside of us. They have been inside all along. We've just disconnected from this truth. One reason why children are so carefree and joyous is because they know they are being taken care of by their parents. Have you ever seen a chronically angry or anxious child? Chances are they are that way because they don't feel as though they have a stable, predictable, and safe life. That's what spirituality is. It's knowing that we are being taken care of no matter what. We can create that safe life for ourselves by re-programming our minds into having faith. If we realize we are safe and supported in everything we do, our fears wash away. Young children have little to worry about because they typically have had no reason to. We can revert back to that feeling by starting again and trusting the process of life. What is there to really be afraid of if we know that everything is unfolding the way it's supposed to?

If you believe that everything happens for a reason, then you have a spiritual platform to work with. Alcoholics Anonymous in itself is a popular and effective program that is based on spiritual practices. People like to criticize spiritual beliefs. It's become a hot topic. People have so many reasons to tear down others' beliefs. Some contest it because they feel bitter about the things that have happened to them. Where was God then? I've had people question my beliefs more times than I can count, and I simply brush it off because it's really none of their business anyways. Your spiritual beliefs or lack thereof are personal and your own business. However, I would be doing readers a great injustice if I didn't share what has not only worked for me, but is by far my number one tool in abandoning anxiety. Knowing that God has my back and that everything around me is happening for a reason has comforted me through my most difficult moments. I know I am supported and my dreams and desires are supported too. I know that when shit hits the fan in my life, it's all part of a perfect plan.

Now, I know that your spiritual or religious beliefs may be different than mine. You can still apply this chapter to your belief system. For the purpose of this book, I'm going to use God because that's my personal belief. I don't judge anyone for their beliefs. I think that's the most epic downfall of religions, and it's not always just religions either. It often is other spiritual practices and other cultures as well. We tend to not accept others' differences and judge, especially if we're feeling uncomfortable or disagree with something somebody is saying.

So, let's talk about God. I want to talk about the importance of spirituality and having a spiritual connection. Like I said, I know this can be an incredibly touchy subject for some people. I can actually relate. Let me explain. When I was a teenager, I used to go to church regularly. My grandparents would take me. When my grandfather died, I kept going for about a year or two and then I pretty much stopped. For some reason, I'm sensitive when it comes to church. I find it really hard to feel comfortable in a church. I'm sure many of you can relate. I feel like I'm being judged. It's something I've had to work on and to be honest, haven't completely mastered yet. I've had people within the church make comments and judge me in the past and it hurt deeply. For some reason, it seems to hurt more when it comes from people in a church. I think it's because we feel like church should be a safe place. We feel like we should be safe from judgment and feel comfortable. That's really the last feeling I would use to describe my churchgoing experiences.

Let's make one thing clear, the actions made by some people in churches to ostracize, judge, and criticize others have nothing to do with God. In fact, the purpose of the church is to be inclusive and encourage everyone to have a relationship with God. I had to remember that no matter how I felt about church or the people in it, I had to focus on the fact that it was not God's fault. One of the misconceptions is to draw away from God because of people. However, people only know what they know with the information they have. People are just people. We screw up, make mistakes, and judge others. We say mean things and do mean things, but we should never blame God for that. Unfortunately, people miss out on a lot of incredible things by not having a spiritual relationship with God because of other people's actions.

Spirituality and religion are complicated because people don't always fall into a category and there are a lot of labels in religion. Some people can identify with a certain religion, but others feel like they can't because they have had some bad experiences with them in the past. Some spiritual people don't like to be called religious and some religious people don't like to be called spiritual. This issue is more concerned with labels, not concepts and essentially is not at all what is important. The importance is to open your mind up to believe in something again. Perhaps you have a belief system. If you do, this chapter will help you tap into that system and learn how to truly surrender and trust it. I learned how to do that during one of the most challenging times of my life.

It was October 2014. I hadn't slept at all in three days. I was on my second month of sleeping patterns like this. I'd wake up, if you can even call it waking up, and sit on my couch at 5:00 am trying to talk myself into getting ready to exercise. Yes, there was a time in my life that no matter what, I would have to exercise hard. No excuses. I'd workout for an hour, shower, obsessively plan all my meals for the day, go to work, come home at lunch, and go back to work again. I would come home and collapse. I'd cry hysterically, curl up in a ball for 15 minutes, rinse, and repeat. It was the most vicious of cycles. It was torture. I knew I couldn't go on like that. I was sad and felt like I was being tortured in a prison, but I was doing it to myself. I was living every single moment of my life in fear. I didn't know what five minutes free of fear looked, felt, or smelled like. Every thought was consumed by fear. I was dead but still breathing. I was dead, but my heart was beating so fast it was practically making an imprint on my t-shirt. I had jet-black dark circles under my eyes and walked around as if I were intoxicated, bumping into things and even smashing up my car. I was the definition of burnout with chronic insomnia.

I remember on one of those days, I was scrolling mindlessly on social media. My friend had this cute little picture pop up on her page that said, "Five minutes of stillness a day will change your life" - May Cause Miracles. For some reason, I liked the sound of that. This quote hit me hard. I thought, "That sounds easy." Five minutes was a time I could embrace. I don't know why this little graphic caught my attention so much, but it did. "'May Cause Miracles,' what does that mean?" I thought. Is it a book? Is it a program? So, I did what every person in my shoes would do. I googled it.

As I stared mindlessly at my phone, a book popped up. The author was Gabrielle Bernstein. "Okay, I'll go buy it this week," I thought. I love buying books. I closed the computer and went on with my day. I decided to head over to my mom's house to distract me a bit from my chronic exhaustion. She was lying in her bed when I arrived. I jumped in beside her and lay down my desperate head. "I'm never going to fall asleep. I've been up for three days, mom," I said with tears flowing continuously down my cheeks onto the pillow. "I just can't! Why is God torturing me like this? Doesn't he know that I have to sleep?" I was in my twenties and felt like I was seventy. I'd been through hell in my life, but there were very few times I could remember feeling this scared. My bed and 10:00 pm were the two scariest things to me. I was afraid of the dark again just like I was when I was a child. Only this time, I was scared that I wouldn't fall asleep. My mom assured me I would be OK as I got up to grab some tissues. When I was in her bathroom, my eyes wandered over to the counter.

"May Cause Miracles" was sitting there. I was shocked to see it. Clearly, it was meant to be. God had put that book there for me. Little did I know, this book would literally change my entire life. I brought it home that night and read the introduction and cried. That night, I went to bed and fell fast asleep. I slept for ten hours for the first time in a year.

That is what you call "synchronicity."

Synchronicity is what psychologist, Carl Jung, describes as "meaningful coincidences." To me, I describe them as just plain miraculous and cool. I realized then that miracles are real, practical, and happen all around us, but the challenge is whether we actually notice the beauty of them or not. The question is not, are they occurring? The question is, do we see them? Do we believe in them? Einstein once said, "We can choose to view life as though nothing is a miracle, or as though everything is a miracle." Do we see miracles, or do we only see the material world around us? The book "A Course in Miracles," talks about how a miracle occurs every time you have a change of perception that moves from fear to love, which is basically from *anxious mind* to *authentic mind*. Every moment you change your perception from *anxious* to *authentic mind*, a miracle occurs.

When it comes to your own spirituality, I want you to notice what feels right for you. Some people who go to church don't believe in swearing or dancing. Those aren't necessarily my beliefs, but it doesn't mean that it's any of my business to tell anyone what makes sense and what doesn't. Religion and spirituality are so unique and individual. As I've said before, we tend to put too many labels on these kinds of things instead of just doing what feels right to us. It's the feelings inside of our hearts that we experience. That's the reason why spirituality is something people are drawn towards. It's not the terrible judgments we toss around at each other. My best advice for you is to do what feels good in your heart. You will know what is for you. Know that spirituality can be your number one tool in your recovery and that alone is worth exploring. I've always been so careful not to force my religion or beliefs on others, but I also feel compelled to share what it did for me and my life. I feel more joy and peace now than I ever have before.

Now, some of you may already have a spiritual daily practice, and that's great. I want to teach you to utilize it as your main resource to aid in your anxiety. First of all, I want you to start considering what your prayers sound like. As there are no wrong ways to pray, I think it may be helpful to shift your perception around your prayers and start asking God what it is you need to learn from your anxiety. Often when we begin to learn the life lessons that diseases or disorders are here to teach us, they start to fade away. Ask God to give you a miracle. Tell him you believe in miracles, and then believe in them with all your heart. Believe like it's your full-time job. I want you to spend a majority of your prayers talking to him about the many things you are so incredibly grateful for. These things can be as simple as the ability to walk when you know others can't. Name your anxiety and own it, then surrender it to the best of your ability and ask God to remove it. Watch for the miracles and life lessons that start to occur, because they will.

Surrendering your fears to a higher power can be easy or difficult. You choose the way. The practice of surrender takes time and major repetition for anxiety sufferers. My favorite visualization is of God saying to me "Please, don't worry, I've got this!" I saw it online once and it really stuck with me. He has our backs. The more I surrender to him, and truly give my worries to him, the more they have transformed miraculously in my life. I could, and probably will one day, write an entire book on how this practice has transformed my life. Don't underestimate the power of your spiritual practice. Make it a daily habit. Do it every morning and every night. You will literally experience miracles the more you trust and release.

Gratitude

Gratitude is a spiritual, practical, and immeasurably powerful mind shifting tool. Gratitude has shifted my anxiety so many times and saved me from going down the rabbit hole of panic and circular thinking. It stops *anxious mind* directly in its tracks. Gratitude is so powerful at strengthening the *authentic mind*, that *anxious mind* can't co-exist with gratitude. When you choose to be grateful, you are fully immersed in *authentic mind*. If you're confused on whether or not you're in a place of *anxious* or *authentic mind*, get grateful. In fact, when it doubt, get grateful.

It's one of my favorite tools because it's so universal and can easily be applied quickly to any situation. It works when you're down, when you're confused, when you're exhausted, when you're scared, when you're defeated and even when you're angry. Getting grateful when you're in doubt of anything can turn around your entire attitude and energy. If you're tired and you get grateful, all of a sudden you have more energy and you feel more awake. When you're angry at someone or something and you get grateful, you will feel more forgiving and calm. Gratitude shifts your energy from negative to positive in one quick second. So why not try getting grateful about everything? Yes, everything. Get grateful for your worry and anxiety too and know it's a victory to have these obstacles in your life and to be able to work through them.

You can choose the type of lens in which you view the world. You always have a choice when it comes to the filter in which you see through. You can look through a filter of awe that lives in curiosity and wonder. You can also look through the filter of defeat that lives in difficulty and depression. This filter can cause you to feel like the world is a hostile place. Choose to see the world in a way that you want to see. You control what you see, therefore you also control your experiences of situations.

There are abundant opportunities to grow and learn daily. You may feel as though you're in a good place and don't have much to learn. Trust me, you still do. We are never done learning, growing, and morphing into better versions of ourselves. Gratitude is an essential part of growth. If you want your dreams and desires to become a reality, start the practice of gratitude first. Start to notice what you do have, and then getting what you want and reaching your personal and mental goals will become much easier.

Chapter 18
Dreams and Desires

Don't let your dreams die just because you have anxiety.

Y ou can make a choice to have a different life no matter what you've been through or who you have been in the past. This is one of my absolute favorite parts of my practice. It is rewarding to talk with people who feel like they have no hope and then watch them transform into dreamers. I love hearing about my clients and their new rewarding careers, places they are traveling to, and all the things they are doing that they never thought they could do. The whole point of having these dreams and desires is to truly experience and feel life. We want to feel accomplished, overjoyed, and genuinely excited. We want to reconnect with our *authentic minds* and our *authentic* selves. We want to feel a childlike excitement for life. The good news is we can feel that way again. You can get genuinely excited about your life.

I was incredibly lost when I first started with my personal coach. I was barely getting to work every day, getting no sleep, and feeling as though I would never be happy again. I was at a loss. I couldn't imagine feeling joy and excitement. How could I? I hadn't felt that kind of happiness in years. I couldn't remember the last time I truly felt that way. I lived and breathed pain my whole life. Something like feeling joy or genuinely excited to wake up every morning, seemed so far out of reach. However, when I started with my coach, I felt encouraged. She seemed to understand what I was going through and could relate to me. I finally found someone who had been through the type of pain I had. She wasn't like the other therapists I had seen. She had been there and got out on the other side, stronger and more successful than I could've ever imagined. It was inspiring to me and gave me hope, yet I was still skeptical on whether I could succeed. I figured I had nothing to lose and put my heart and soul into my recovery.

Within four months, I was living out my lifelong dream. I wanted to see Los Angeles. I have always been obsessed with film and wanted to see where it all happened. I will never forget the image of myself joyously running under the pier in Santa Monica, literally with tears in my eyes because I couldn't believe that this was my life. I couldn't fathom the joy and freedom I was feeling. I felt like a child, wild and free walking barefoot in the sand while the waves crashed beneath me and the sun set in California. The moment was perfect, but what was even more perfect was that I felt my anxiety slip away. It was literally gone for four days. I had the odd *anxious* thought but noticed I was able to casually dismiss it as being a lie and not my true *authentic* mind. I knew and understood what was going on, and I wasn't going to give my *anxious mind* power anymore. From there, everything started to fall into place. I was experiencing these moments more often in my daily life. I started to see the possibilities for myself. It was like the light at the end of my long, cold, dark tunnel.

These moments of excitement and joy became more frequent and slowly started to last longer than the thoughts of my *anxious mind.* I was beginning to live my life within the *authentic mind* and it felt like nothing I had ever felt before. I had never experienced this. I couldn't believe how natural it began to feel. Each day, I was getting closer to freedom. It was actually attainable for me, even though I never thought this was possible. How could this be? I have a chemical imbalance. How could I feel so normal? How could I be happier than my "normal" friends? This was my lifelong dream and I was in it. I was living it.

I only have one rule for people when they begin to think about their dreams. It must be something that gets you excited. It doesn't have to be reachable, attainable or realistic. Your dreams have likely happened for other people, so what makes you different from them? You are not more or less important than the people who have reached the goals you have for yourself. The main difference I see between the people who live out their dreams and the people who don't is dedication and the ability to pursue and not give up. "Don't give up on your dreams." We have heard these phrases so often that we have become immune to them, but they are still true. Don't become immune to these powerful pieces of advice. Allow yourself to get excited about your life. Eat, sleep and breathe your dreams. Become obsessed with them.

I also want to touch on a common misconception society has about having dreams and being a certain age. We often feel that once we graduate high school, the next step is to go to college. After college, society expects us to go get a reliable and predictable job that we may or may not be overly passionate about. If you're not laughing and smiling every day at your job and excited to get there in the mornings, you may want to reevaluate things. We work for a majority of our lives, so we may as well be doing something we are obsessed with and that we feel pulled to do, not pushed to do. Honestly, who decided that our dreams should become unrealistic at a certain age? This has always bothered me. No one should decide what age you should be doing what. Having standards on one another like that only creates judgment, disappointment and feelings of failure. It's your life. You make the rules - not your family, friends, or society. Every person is different, so every life and timeline will be different too.

Our desires and dreams are ours for a reason. We develop our dreams from specific interests and talents that are totally unique to us. Your dreams are meant to be yours. I believe this with my whole heart. Everything happens for a reason and so do the dreams and desires we have within us. When we can get truly excited about something, that excitement is an indication that we are on the right track. We need to push through and keep pursuing that excitement and vision. One thing I suggest to my clients is be very careful who you tell your dreams to. People mean well, but people like to crap all over your dreams. I apologize for the graphic description, but it's very true. They live in fear, base every decision on fear, and are totally unaware of it. Forgive them, but don't listen to or hang around them. You need to focus on your recovery and your dreams. You don't have time for other people's opinions, especially opinions of people who are not even living the life you want.

We go into more depth about dreams in the 40-day program. This program will provide you with some next steps in pursuing and getting into the mindset of your dreams.

Chapter 19

Powerful Mindset Tools to Support You

Behavioral changes aren't always easy. In fact, they are almost always challenging. However, behavioral changes can also be rewarding and enjoyable. I actually enjoyed the process of recovery from my anxiety because I knew these behavioral changes were permanent. I wasn't putting a temporary fix on my anxiety, I was changing the way my mind worked. You can enjoy these behavioral changes too. You can look forward to practicing the tools within this book and the 40 Day Program. Your behavior and lifestyle changes are imperative to your recovery.

If you think about it, it's kind of ridiculous for us to be so addicted to struggling that we dread any form of change. These changes are good and are things I could never imagine living my life without. I legitimately get excited about my life and many of these tools are the reasons why. Get rid of the struggle, because the struggle is only adding drama to your life where there doesn't have to be. Let's look at some strategies you can start using today to support you in your recovery.

Morning Routine

Take a look at your morning routine. What does it look like? How do you feel in the mornings? Years ago, my routine was pretty depressing. It was: hit the alarm clock, go back to sleep, hit it again, go back to sleep for those precious "ten more minutes," and then reluctantly roll out of bed, exhausted. I'd usually complain to my husband about how I barely slept and how I didn't know how I was going to get through the day. I'd eat, get ready, drag myself out the door, and throw on my sunglasses. I remember how my co-workers always used to tell me how hungover I looked when I came into work. This was not the best way to get my day started. I went on like this for years until my friend and meditation expert, George Peterson, introduced me to his new morning routine, which was based on the book, "The Miracle Morning."

Funny enough, I had just walked past the book in my naturopathic doctor's office earlier that same day and considered buying it, which was not a coincidence. Everything happens for a reason. George and I committed to doing the program together for thirty days and the results were truly transformational. I haven't stopped since. Waking up just a bit earlier and starting my days off in a positive and excited way, changed my life.

It's so important to note how you're starting your days off. It's a very good indicator of how the rest of your day will go. You will notice a difference if you wake up dreading the day or if you're excited for it. It will make a difference whether you take the time to meditate in the morning or wait until your day is heading in a downwards spiral to do it. Start your mornings off properly and don't wait for your body to crave peace. Give your mind and body what it needs as soon as you wake up. Start a new daily morning routine that you can really get excited about.

In my 40-day program, at the end of the book, I structure your morning routines for you. For now, I want you to begin to open your mind to waking up a bit earlier and changing those morning routines for the sake of your anxiety recovery.

The Power of Affirmations

One of my favorite tools for personal growth and trying to move to the next level in my life is affirmations. Affirmations are positive phrases that you say out loud. They help to condition your mind and are part of a full immersion healing process. Remember cramming for a major history test in school? You probably walked around your bedroom with your textbook in hand citing off dates and facts out loud in hopes you would remember them. Affirmations are similar in that you are trying to teach your mind to remember these statements so you can get them into your psyche. It is likened unto a brainwashing process. An example of an affirmation would be "I am unstoppable, powerful and strong."

I'm a big fan of affirmation apps because they can pop up on your cellphone throughout the day. I like to set mine to "random" so I don't know which one I'm going to get. When my affirmations pop up on my phone, I say them out loud 3 times. I try and take a minute to close my eyes and take one deep breath in afterward. I find this the absolute most effective way to get the messages into my subconscious mind. It just reinforces messages to your *authentic mind* in a way nothing else does.

Importance of Making Decisions

We talked about intuition earlier and now I want to talk about how important it is for people with anxiety to make and commit to decisions. I believe using your intuition and gut feelings are very important in the decision-making process. Decision-making can be very hard for anxious people. I see it all the time. We are constantly worrying about outcomes and making a choice is hard. When my anxiety was at its peak, it would take me hours and hours to pack for an overnight trip and shopping was an anxiety nightmare. I swear I used to spend hours shopping for clothes going back and forth on each item again and again. Even picking the right fruit used to stress me out! I was obsessively making pro/con lists and never ever wanted to "fail," or make the wrong choice. Inside my head, I truly believed something terrible would always happen if I did.

I'm here to tell you that nothing horrible will happen and that there really isn't a wrong choice to make. If you knew that every choice you made was the right choice, how would you make your choices? We need to start understanding that everything happens for a reason. If you make the "wrong" choice, it really isn't the wrong one if you're making it from your heart. You either make the right choice or you learn from it. Our *anxious minds* convince us that no matter what choice we make, it'll be the wrong one. The *anxious mind* tells us that life will end and the world as we know it will implode if we decide the wrong thing. *Anxious mind* puts a lot of pressure on us to make the "right" choice. What if we switched our thoughts around and understood the truth that we really can't screw up? Think about how much easier it would be to make choices.

Getting into a place of inspiration can help you make important decisions that come from *authentic mind* vs *anxious mind. Authentic mind* thrives in a place of inspiration. Inspiration feels refreshing and confident. Sometimes we go away for a week or so, change up our surroundings, relax and enjoy ourselves, and we feel more inspired than ever. We often feel inspired to set new goals and make changes. When we return home, maybe we keep those commitments for a week or so, but then we regress. This is because *anxious mind* takes over. You return to reality and separate from inspiration. When we are inspired, we get creative too. Often we shut off our creativity because we are so immersed in the everyday stressors of life. Experiment with the things and places that inspire you and set aside more time for them.

Some things that inspire me are:

- Going outside and grounding myself
- Going to my favorite places
- Seeing a great movie with a powerful message
- Going to a play or concert
- Connecting with good people

Journal Entry

Pull out your journal now and write down two choices you feel you need to make. Write down things and places that inspire you. Even if they are places you don't get the opportunity to go to very often, write them down. How can you incorporate these places and things into your daily life? How do you feel when you are surrounded by inspiration? How can you feel inspired more regularly? Getting inspired will help you make those choices. Just be patient, the answers will come.

Changing Your Story

We must understand that we are new people now and we have the power to create a new story for ourselves. We can change our rules and create a new life. When I was a teenager, I remember feeling the pressure of packing for family vacations. Due to my OCD, packing was incredibly stressful for me. I never wanted to forget anything and thought if I did, something terrible would happen. I would get majorly stressed out about packing too much and not being able to fit it in the car. I knew if I packed too much, I was no doubt going to hear a lot of comments about it from my family and that shot my anxiety through the roof. I would try and stuff as much as I could into one bag and anxiously try and fit it into the car before anyone else would see. Of course, someone would always see and inevitably make a comment about it. There was no avoiding it. It wasn't their fault either. They didn't understand the way my mind worked.

When we would arrive at our destination, arguing would inevitably follow. Don't get me wrong, some of my best childhood memories are from family vacations, but they were also incredibly stressful. When I told my coach about these experiences, she helped me to realize that I had taken these limiting beliefs about vacations being stressful into adulthood. Even though my husband couldn't care a less how much I packed, I always stressed out about it and tried to sneak my bags into the car, just like I did as a child. My coach pointed out something life-changing to me. She said, "You're a new person now. You can't unlearn what you already know. It's time to change your story around vacations." She also told me that it was my birthright to go off and enjoy a calming vacation with my husband. I didn't have to earn a vacation. I didn't have to make it a once a year special thing either. I make the rules now. I can recreate my story. I don't have to put so much pressure on myself to enjoy vacations because I can go on a vacation whenever I want. She taught me how to not only take the pressure off, but also to see it through my new eyes. I don't have to repeat the same story.

The same thing applies for every area of life. You don't need to repeat family patterns or your own patterns anymore. You are a new person having a new experience. You decide how your story goes. Understanding this important mindset tool can help further weaken the "mindset" leg of the tripod.

Conditioning Ourselves

Conditioning our minds is basically what exposure therapy is. In exposure therapy, we start small, expose ourselves to a fear, and slowly work up to tougher challenges. It conditions and reprograms the mind from interpreting something as fearful to interpreting it as safe. We have to remember we have the strong ability to condition our minds and we do it daily, whether we notice it or not. The difference is, we don't often condition ourselves to become the people we need to be.

Re-conditioning the mind is not as difficult as you think. When trying to rid yourself of negative habits, you can remember there was likely a time when you didn't need them. You've conditioned your mind to thrive on these negative routines but not necessarily on the positive ones. The truth is, there is no order of difficulty here. It's not easier or more difficult to continue bad habits as opposed to good ones. Take quitting smoking for instance. Quitting is made to be this big scary thing. As smokers, we are told that when you quit, it will be like your own personal Armageddon. Life as you know it will come crashing down around you. You will be nervous, anxious, and unable to sleep or function like you did when you were on the drug. People love to share their own personal horror stories. "OMG, all my hair fell out, I couldn't sleep and I ate everything in sight. I even tried to eat my own child when I quit smoking!" I've heard it all, trust me.

Do we ever stop for a minute and challenge these thoughts? For me, quitting smoking was in no way the most difficult thing I've ever done. In fact, it was one of the simplest things I ever did. The point is, would all of these people have had such an incredibly hard time quitting smoking if they didn't hear about all the other horror stories people told them? Did they have preconceived notions about the quitting process? We need to understand that we don't need bad things but we DO need to set aside time for the good. Condition yourself for greatness and know that it's not as hard as you think. You've conditioned yourself for many negative habits, now do the same with things that will benefit you. Conditioning takes time and consistency.

Switch Up Your Focus

Switching things up and "shocking your system," is a good way to let out your anxious energy. When you switch what you're focusing on, your mind doesn't have time to catch up with your body and sometimes that's a good thing. I find this to be a fun and interesting tool to use. When you get into a place of *anxious mind* and circular thinking, I always suggest first tackling "The Five Senses of Peace." Some other great ways in which to shock your system and change what you're focusing on are body movements. When I'm in a place of constant fear, I like to throw on music and dance. Not just a normal dance. I love to dance crazy. I have a CD player or iPod and some speakers always set up in my house. I find it to be an easy and quick way to change up my focus. Sometimes this looks like closing all the doors, blaring music, and dancing all your energy out. You may be thinking "dancing can't be a real suggestion," because let's face it, no one really feels like dancing when they're having depression or anxiety. That's actually the whole point. You are not giving your mind and body what it expects. You're shocking it. Sometimes you just have to muster up the strength and energy, and for us, it takes a lot of strength and energy to get off the couch and out of your pajamas, but we must.

We need to get up, get dressed, turn on music, and dance. Sometimes, changing your focus can simply mean a five minute walk outside, while you repeat a mantra. Once, I got up and did exactly that as it was pouring rain outside. I was committed to doing anything that would help me, including running and crying in the rain. Shock your body by changing your routine. Get up.

Laughter is another really great way to change up your focus. Have you ever been super anxious and then saw something hilarious? It completely shocks your system. The point is, find something that works for you and repeat it 20 times a day if you have to.

Ways to switch things up when you're in the midst of anxious thoughts:

- music
- dance
- running
- kickboxing
- yoga
- tai chi
- chi gong

"Just Stop Worrying"

One of my all-time favorite things that I have heard people say over the years is, "Just stop worrying about it." I'm making a sarcastic statement, in case you didn't know. People mean well. They really do, but they just don't get it. They have good intentions, and we must understand this as anxiety sufferers. People who don't suffer from anxiety truly don't get it and we have to remember that we can't expect them too. They haven't been in our minds and thoughts, and they really believe they are helping in telling us to just stop worrying. Despite their good intentions, this phrase does nothing for us. We are still worried about whatever we were told to stop worrying about. Nothing changes after we are told this and in fact, it usually just makes us feel helpless.

There is an answer to this issue of worry though and the key is to change your perspective. When you actually change your perspective, and look at things in a different way, you really can genuinely let it go. The most important piece here is that you need to actually change your mind about it and believe it. You can't fake your thoughts. You can't just pretend to have changed your mind or perspective, you have to actually convince yourself. For example, my husband and I were taking a walk by our house one day and my *anxious mind* took over. I could barely notice any of the beautiful scenery around me. I was obsessing about the next step I was taking in my life by quitting my job. I was talking it over with him and no matter what we did that day, no matter how nice it was outside, I could only see my fear. I couldn't shut my mind off.

This was a feeling I was all too familiar with. This was my story since childhood. I never really knew how to stop these circular thinking patterns in their tracks. My anxiety always sucked me in at the worst of times. I would try and redirect myself, distract myself, and constantly tell myself to stop worrying. I repeatedly told myself that worrying about it wouldn't solve the problem. Still, I was obsessing. When we stopped by a store, my husband turned and said to me, "If I tell you to stop worrying, that's not going to do anything for you. You won't feel any better until you see this differently, really change your perspective, and become OK with it. Become excited about it." That's when a lightbulb went off for me. There was no need to just keep telling myself to stop worrying. I had to see the entire situation differently. I needed to see that whatever happened in my job, it was not the end for me. This was actually an exciting beginning. If I quit and I go broke, I'm not dying. I'm still alive and it's just paving the way for better things in my life. Was I happy at my current job? No. So, how could quitting be a bad thing? It was a whole new change in perspective. I saw the situation in a whole new light. See, once I saw things differently, and I changed how I viewed this predicament of "to quit or not to quit," I felt calm. I felt like I couldn't make the "wrong" choice. I felt better inside my heart and inside my head. I actually began to feel excited, and I couldn't fake that feeling either. I had to convince myself fully that I was embarking on an exciting beginning.

I ended up following my heart and it worked out. Now, I run a business helping people free themselves from their own anxiety and circular thinking.

If the Thing I Fear Happens, Let It Happen

This is a powerful mindset tool. We give our fears a lot of power even though they are just False Evidence Appearing Real (FEAR). Unfortunately, it's the "appearing real" part that's really hard for us suffering from anxiety because it really does feel so real, even though it's not. Our fears are lies that our *anxious mind* tells us. The more we believe it, the more we feed the *anxious mind*. I love to do this exercise when faced with a really crippling fear. I like to go to the fear within my mind, or write it down and dismantle it one by one. Then, I like to really get into my head and keep asking myself, "What is the worst that can possibly happen?" I would write down reasons why it's incredibly illogical and then become OK with the worst possible outcome. Nine times out of ten, when you step back and look at the fear and the worst possible outcome, you can get yourself to a place of acceptance.

We try so hard to control all outcomes in our lives, when in reality, that's impossible. I used to do outlandish things to make sure outcomes turned out the way I wanted them to. I'd go to great lengths to control them, and guess what? The more I tried to neurotically control things in my life, the worse the outcomes became. I used to intricately plan things, because I was so afraid of things going badly. I would plan down to the last minute, literally sucking out all the joy, fun, and spontaneity of life. Also, the more I tried to control my desired outcome, the more stressed out I got. When I finally realized this, I released it. Our car would break down, the hotel room would flood (yes this happened), and unexpected financial obligations would pop up out of nowhere. When I finally adopted a more relaxed mindset of "everything happens for a reason," and accepted that even if my plans got derailed, I would survive, the more life just started to work out. Things came up for sure. I still had obstacles I had to face, but I didn't stress about them anymore.

I remember being tested one day on my trip to Boston. It was my first trip in some time and I packed my carry-on wrong. I basically didn't read the fine print when I ordered my ticket online and put all my toiletries in my carry-on bag. Airport security ended up taking all of them from me before my flight, but I stayed calm. After getting off the phone with my mother later that day, I told her what happened at the airport. She was shocked by my ability to handle it so well. "Wow," she said. "One year ago if that happened, it would have sent you off the rails." She was right. I was doing much better.

The fact is, the more stress you bring to a situation and the more fear and worry you feed your *anxious mind*, the less fun your *authentic mind* can have. Trust me, the *authentic mind* feeds on fun. This is the whole point, too. If you're not having fun, what's the point really?

When the worst thing that can happen no longer scares you, that's when you know you are healing on a massive level. The likelihood of your "worst possible outcome" coming true is almost always around 1%. Don't waste your life obsessing about 1%. In fact, the less you worry, the less likely it will happen. Sit back and know everything happens for a reason and that you are supported on your journey.

When You Find Something that Works for You, Take Note of It.

One of my clients adores movies and film and it's the only time he can relax because it's a huge passion for him. Other people find watching movies challenging, especially in theaters. The point is that nothing will be the same for two people. When you know something works, write it down. We all have our conventional and unconventional places of joy. The thing is, the further you go along in your road to recovery, the more you will begin to understand what things inspire you and bring you peace and what doesn't. Take note of these things. Write them down. I actually have one journal specifically for this purpose. Whenever I'm feeling down, stuck, or alone, I turn to this journal. It is literally pages and pages of things that have worked for me and places that inspire me. It quickly shifts my perspective back to my *authentic mind*. It's important to find and explore your own personal outlet as well. This can be creative movement or just something fun that you enjoy doing.

Some great examples are:

- Dance

- Write

- Karate

- Kickboxing

- Rapping

- Singing

Find something that helps you, not anyone else. Once you find your unique outlet, you'll know what it is. Don't just follow in the footsteps of what the people around you find acceptable or normal. Embrace your own unique interests and go try something you've always wanted to try. Experiment with what helps to bring you back to that place of inspiration.

Chapter 20
Changing Your Home to Support You

Changing our home environment to support us in our recovery can make a huge difference. I can't tell you how important it is to have a supportive home and work environment around you when you suffer from anxiety and depression. When I moved houses and changed my work environment around, I felt the positive change instantly. The following are some things you can do at home to help support you in your recovery.

Lighting

Changing a light bulb in your home or in your workplace can have a huge impact on your stress. We are very sensitive people in the anxiety/OCD/depression community. We can be sensitive to light, clothing material, tags on our clothes and a myriad of other things, but let's talk about light. Having LED lights is the new environmental trend. Almost every store and place you go to these days has them. They are great for saving energy and also great for the environment, but not so much for our anxious eyes and bodies. They emit a strong almost piercing bright, white light. This light rarely has any warmth and has more of a blue/cold feel to it, which is not great for anxious eyes.

Fluorescent lights are the same. These are the lights most commonly used in hospitals, schools and discount stores. Why? They are cheap. I've had many conversations with parents about the lights in the schools and how bad they are for learning. When I worked for the school board, I would religiously turn out all or most of the lights in the classrooms and instantly observe the anxious children calm down. This is a simple and not so obvious solution but I found it was profound. The lights may be cheap and energy efficient, but they can totally kill your calm vibe and make you very irritable and more likely to become anxious and depressed. Now, if it is important for you to have the LED light bulbs for cost and energy savings, make sure you buy LED bulbs that are rated at 2700 lumens. These specific LED bulbs emulate the soft warm glow of the halogen bulbs.

I also love dimmers. After I installed dimmers in literally every room in my house and changed out the LEDs, it helped me settle into my body so much more. I could actually feel my body respond and softly settle back into my shoulders. My breath even softened.

Clearing Out the Stuff

This had a substantial impact on my energy while at home. The reason I'm telling you to get rid of your stuff is it can really have an effect on your mood. Clearing out old clothes you don't adore, objects you're only hanging onto out of fear that "it may be useful someday," or any random stuff you just don't use, can be incredibly therapeutic. I want to challenge each of you to rid yourself of one bag full of stuff right after reading this. I know this can be hard for us to do, especially if you have hoarding issues, which can be very common with OCD. If this is an uncontrollable trigger for you, you can wait until it starts to feel more natural to complete this task without pressure.

The Japanese people try to keep their spaces as empty as possible. The reason for this is peace. Clutter is chaos. Clearing out stuff allows you to relax and breathe more. It provides a more supportive and expansive space to heal. You know what I'm talking about. You know how hotels and spas always have that minimalistic atmosphere that just makes it a bit easier to unwind and relax in? I can guarantee those places would not have the calming effects that we love if there were clutter and useless stuff everywhere in sight. It would not be peaceful jumping into a hot tub and having to step over a bunch of trinkets that were knocked into the water as you were getting in. Marie Kondo explains it best, "Take each item in one's hand and ask; "Does this spark joy? If it does, keep it: if not, dispose of it." This can also help you to start fresh and begin a new chapter in your life since you WILL get better.

Keeping the house tidy touches on the clutter issue as well. You would be shocked what cleaning your house does to your mood and anxiety. Having dirt on all your floors and dust all over your tables doesn't make for a positive environment where you can really thrive in your journey towards peace. This is why it's so important to get rid of all the junk in your house and de-clutter. It makes it so much easier to clean and we need all the help we can get. Make it easy on yourself. Set yourself up for success in all areas and make your house easy to clean by ditching the clutter.

Play Music

I like to play jazz and calming music on low in the background in my house. My friends seem to think that makes me a 70-year-old man, but it's just what I like. Having calming music really changes up the atmosphere in the house, especially at night.

However, you can really play whatever music you want. So often we forget to play music in our homes. Heal with music, because it's fun.

Scents

Going out and purchasing some essential oils that you love and putting them in a home diffuser is a great way to calm down. It's so important to have comforting smells in your home, so have fun picking them out. If you or anyone in your home currently smokes, make sure to do it outside. When you smoke inside the house, those chemicals linger within the furniture and it's important for your sleep and anxiety to have clean, crisp air flowing through at all times. Opening up the windows is also important for regular air circulation.

Set Your Home Up the Way YOU Want To

Don't do anything because of what others may think or comment on. If you want to paint your living room bright orange and have white Christmas lights inside all year round, then do it! Remember, you are the one who has to live in your home. Don't set your home up to impress anyone but yourself. Set it up in ways that reflect your personality and bring you to a place of calm. I personally like to make my house fun by bringing some stuff in from my childhood. Next thing on my to-do list at home is to make a treehouse. Yes, I said it.

Chapter 21
Helping Others and Paying it Forward

I believe we are put on this earth to make a difference in the lives of others. I also believe we go through the experiences and challenges we do so that we can overcome them and teach others how to do the same. Anxiety sufferers are naturally empathetic people. It's one of our super powers. We understand the darkness others have gone through, having gone through it ourselves. This has been my own personal passion since I can remember. I have always wanted to help people for a living. I've wanted to make a massive impact since I was a child. I had a dream in middle school that I would one day open a hotel for homeless people. Maybe one day I will.

As anxiety sufferers, we have a responsibility to the rest of the world. We have a responsibility to help and love people through their pain. We have gone through these times of darkness to learn, grow, and ultimately be a guide for others to help them rise up. We don't want others to feel the way we have felt. It's time to find a way of passing the messages from this book on to those who need it. Maybe we share this book with others, go to online support groups and help others there, or do what I did and create a career around it. We have an opportunity to share how we freed ourselves from our pain. This is actually the best way for us to heal ourselves. It gives us a motivation and a drive to serve the world in a way many others can't. You needed to go through these experiences in order to relate to other people.

"If you're feeling helpless, help someone." - Aung San Suu Kyi

When I'm feeling discouraged, depressed, helpless, and everything in my life seems to be going completely wrong, I quickly remember these words I first heard from Gabby Bernstein quoting Aung San Suu Kyi. This pulls me out of *anxious mind* and into my *authentic mind*. I can't tell you how rewarding it is to help others, especially when you feel down. It's a great tool to switch up what you're focusing on like we spoke about earlier. This doesn't mean you have to push yourself to a place where it feels exhausting. I still want you to keep your boundaries because you are recovering, but helping others when you feel motivated to do so can be quite healing. It's a great way to give back and it also shifts your state at the same time. Usually, if I help someone when I'm in a helpless state myself, I can barely remember why I was so upset to begin with.

I want you to remember this when considering a life of service. I can't reach the audience you can reach just like you can't reach the audience I can reach. We all have a unique story, a unique voice, and unique experiences. These experiences were meant to happen to us so we can relate to and help others. Share your story. You owe it to the people out there suffering, just as I did. There is no competition in this world as far as I'm concerned. We all are a part of the same mission and we need to stay focused on the massive impact we can have in this world. This is our purpose. This is the opportunity for us to become the heroes we never had in our lives. It's true. We can become the heroes we always needed.

With all the hatred going on, we need this movement of love. How can we make a difference as one single person? We can love the hell out of every person we encounter on a daily basis. We must fight the extreme hatred in this world with extreme laughter, extreme love, and extreme peace. Pay it forward and be kind. Know that people have their own stuff they are dealing with. This is how anxiety can be our gift. We need to create a movement where we can teach others to have no shame about their anxiety. I am only one person and I need your help to spread this essential message with the world. We can make a change.

Section Four
40 Day Program

Chapter 22
40-day program

Getting to the end result needs to be both challenging and enjoyable; if you're not enjoying yourself along the way, then what's the point? So now that you've read the book, I have a 40-day outline for you to partake in. 40 is a significant number. Biblically speaking, 40 days is used close to 150 times in the bible. In Hal Elrod's book, "The Miracle Morning," he talks about the significance of 30 days as being a time when you can transform and create a habit. After I completed the 30 day challenge, I decided that I agreed with Hal; however, I felt that people who suffer from anxiety would actually benefit from those extra ten days of further conditioning. We have dealt with so much pain and brainwashing from the *anxious mind* for years, so we could use more time to be patient and re-structure our thoughts.

We are using an immersion process here so you do not feel alone after this book is complete. I've designed the next 40 days for you so we can begin to retrain the mind and re-structure your thoughts and brain chemistry. You are also encouraged to practice the other tools outlined in this book throughout the next 40 days. This is structured to be an immersive experience because frankly, the only way to beat anxiety drug-free is to be immersive. These problems are all-encompassing, so your recovery must be too. Follow the book's instructions for the next 40 days and I can assure you, you will have massive shifts and enjoy yourself during the process.

So why are there only ten days constructed in this chapter? Well, the days are repetitive. The idea is to repeat the ten-day increments over four times. Since repetition plays a vital role in the retraining of the mind, repeating ten days over is the most effective, and it has been designed to deliver.

This 40-day program was designed to weaken "The Tripod of Anxiety" in an intense way. One by one we will dismantle each leg, but it takes consistency. Just like anxiety is persistent, we have to be ten times more persistent. It works. Your freedom is finally right around the corner! You deserve it after everything you've been through.

The days are structured for a time in the morning, midday and evening. I suggest you wake up ten to fifteen minutes earlier than usual to commit to this program. Each day has an affirmation. You are to set this daily affirmation into an affirmation app on your phone. Just make sure you can put your own personalized affirmations in. Set your affirmation to pop up at least once every two hours. The more the better. Checking in three times a day, plus all the times your affirmations pop up on your phone, helps to create an immersive experience.

If you do miss a day or feel as if you want to stay on the same day for a few extra days, go right ahead. As long as you complete at least 40 days, you can lengthen it if you feel the need to. Trust your gut. You will know what is right for you. Don't come down on yourself or abandon the entire program just because you've missed a day. Forgive yourself, be kind and easy on yourself, and pick up right where you left off. Stay committed. The people who get the best and fastest results are the ones who stick to at least 40 days. You can always do the 40 days over again. It was designed for repetition.

"The Five Senses of Peace," was also designed to use over and over again. You will find yourself using "The Five Senses" frequently, especially at the beginning of your healing journey. Be patient, do the work, and stick to it. Sometimes the things in life we need to conquer the most feel repetitive or uncomfortable to start. Just remember, the more resistant you are to it, the more you likely need it. I hated meditation at first. I told myself lies and listened to my *anxious mind*, even though I knew I needed to mediate. Now, I love it. After practice and commitment, it became easy and natural to me. I figured that nothing could be as bad as the hell I was living in. My OCD and anxiety were so hard on my life. I was willing to do whatever it took to heal. Remember that. Nothing is as hard or as challenging as your anxiety. Again, you have nothing to lose and so so much to gain. You can't even see the gains right now, but I can. I know they are there for you and I know that bright light at the end of your tunnel provides opportunities in life you can't even dream up right now. Trust me, this is your time. "The Five Senses" is a tool you will use for the rest of your life. When times are tough, you will use it several times a day. Don't brush this step off. Use it constantly. Use it a hundred times a day if you have to.

I also want to prepare you a bit. Make sure you have a journal. This is a key part to your recovery. You have to want to write in it. It needs to pull you in, not be a chore. Tidy up a space in your house in which you go to do the 40-day program exercises in the morning and at night. This should be a peaceful place and not just your bed or the couch. Tidy up a small corner in a room on the floor where you can sit and comfortably meditate. This place should be uncluttered and as quiet as you can get it. You need to commit to having that 10-15 mins in the morning and that 10-15 mins at night. You can take more time if you'd like to as well. The more time you spend on this, the better. You will also be asked to make a playlist or listen to some older, classic songs during the program. Keep that in mind now and start preparing for that. It will be a playlist from your childhood that brings about positive associations with it and can't be songs you listen to regularly. I wanted to give you that heads up now, so start thinking and creating it.

Another aspect of the 40 day program is the use of technology. Technology, in this case, means TV streaming shows, social media, and time spent texting or online. I am not making strict parameters here. This is all about subtle shifts. The only challenge I have for you is to make a slight and subtle daily change to your use of technology. You decide what that slight change is. Maybe the first thing you do when you wake up is go on your phone to check your emails or social media pages. In that case, you may decide to wait thirty minutes before checking and instead, read the morning exercise of the 40-day program and practice your time of silence and stillness. Perhaps you watch a TV streaming program for three hours every night, but instead you decide to take twenty minutes of that time and go stand outside and look at the stars or take that time to read a chapter in a book. Whatever you decide the challenge is, make sure to make some change daily.

Finally, understand and know that you will have times of discouragement when you feel as though you are taking steps backwards, and not moving along as quickly as you would like. Your anxiety will not magically vanish. You have to do the work. Part of doing the work is being understanding with yourself and knowing that during those bad days or moments, you can choose *authentic mind* again. You can return back to *authentic mind* anytime you choose. You can choose to view the challenges as a sign that your recovery is moving forward, because that is exactly what is happening. The most discouraging days need to be celebrated, for it just means the *anxious mind* is weakening and sometimes the *anxious mind* wants to get a bit louder so you pay attention to it again. The *anxious mind* can frantically try to grab a reason and weasel its way back in. Your mind and body are SO used to choosing *anxious mind,* that when you start to choose *authentic mind,* it may feel kind of weird. The *anxious mind* will get pissed off at you. Just know that this is a good sign. Tell the *anxious mind* to leave and return to your place of love. Make a point to enjoy this process and understand that your healing is here. You have already made the commitment, and it will happen for you. You will be surprised. It is easier than you think.

Day One: Challenge Your Thoughts Day

Today's Affirmation:
"I am observing my thoughts and actions today. I choose authentic mind."

We begin the next ten days with this very vital and important day. Challenging your thoughts is imperative for having the life you deserve. It is so effective to take a step back and question everything today - thoughts, routines, everything. If you don't observe and notice your thoughts, how can you change them? This is not a step to skip, as you cannot have the form of healing that you long for without it. It is also super important that you do not use today to judge yourself. Remember, we have all been programmed to choose *anxious mind* over *authentic mind*. Today you are observing yourself without any judgment towards yourself or others. I'm making you take a step back and notice your situation. Your response to your *anxious thoughts* throughout today is, "Hmmm that's interesting."

When it comes to observing the thoughts and actions that originate from the *anxious mind*, it can be hard to differentiate between *anxious* and *authentic*. Often we question ourselves and get confused about which place a thought is coming from. With my experience, *the authentic mind* always feels right and good. Here are some great examples of how *anxious mind* takes the wheel in my life, and some things to watch out for today:

- Judgmental thoughts towards yourself or others ("He's an ass. She's so uptight. I look so tired today.")

- Dread ("I'm so exhausted" or "How am I going to get through this day?")

- Pessimism ("I'm never going to feel better." "My life sucks!")

- Complaining

- What If's (What if I never feel better?)

- Lying

- People Pleasing ("No, no worries, it's not a problem!")

- Saying "Yes" when you want to say "NO!"

- Engaging in or listening to gossip

- Not owning your truth (Not expressing your true feelings in a conversation, playing small)

As this is a 40-day experience, if you are on your second, third or fourth round of the ten days, I would like you to not only notice your thoughts and actions but also choose *authentic mind* over *anxious mind*. In order to have lasting change, you must observe but you must also choose a different path. We are reprogramming the mind here, don't forget. The goal is to always be switching from *anxious mind* to *authentic mind*, and when we don't, gently choosing again. You can return back to *authentic mind* anytime you want. Don't ever forget that.

I want you to also consider becoming an outside-of-the-box thinker. Today is the day to challenge not only your thoughts, but your views and opinions of the world around you. See, we have all been brainwashed and programmed into thinking certain things. Take today to reflect on those judgments. Society has brainwashed all of us into thinking certain things are good or bad, normal or abnormal. Certain things make you look like you're crazy, weak, successful, or powerful. Female norms, male norms, we all have accepted these brainwashed ideas and use them so often in our daily lives that we take them as truths without even questioning them.

Question everything. Never stop questioning, it's how we learn and get to know our true selves. We now need to sit back and think about all the limitations we have put on ourselves and others due to this brainwashing. Maybe you are a man who was interested in going to school for visual arts but your father told you it was a woman's career. Or maybe you are a woman who has many male friends and people tell you that you're a flirt. Perhaps we look at the people who don't fit our ideas or norms and we judge them for it. "Oh, he's irresponsible for quitting his job," is a sound example. The bottom line is that there are so many judgments going on in our heads about ourselves and others. So, we must ask ourselves, what if there were no norms? What if we were born into a world where we were free to follow our hearts without hesitation? What would you have done differently? What can we do differently right now? Let's begin to question all the ways in which we've been brainwashed, challenge those thoughts, and start fresh by choosing again.

Morning Exercise:

1. Meditate: All you have to do for this is be totally still, close your eyes and breathe deep, slow breaths. You can mentally repeat this mantra or say it aloud,

   "I observe, I am curious. I observe, I am curious."

   Breathe in and out, long and slow, and have the mantra follow the rhythm of the breath. Do this for 5-10 mins. It doesn't matter if your thoughts drift, just come back to the mantra. Let your body go a little limp at the end and take a big sigh of relief.

2. Pray and release the day out loud:

   "As I go into my day, please guide me to see the things I am meant to see. Help me to understand where my thoughts are coming from and how they are helping or hindering me in my recovery from anxiety. I want to heal. I am willing to do whatever it takes to heal. I am ready to take on today and become curious about my actions and thought patterns without judgment. My job is to observe myself today. I release today to you. Amen."

3. Don't forget to do a daily check in with yourself regarding your technology use. Make one subtle change today.

Midday Exercise:

Around noon or lunchtime, take a minute to check in with yourself, put your hand to your heart, close your eyes and say today's mantra three times.

Today's affirmation to put in your phone and repeat all day long:
"I am observing my thoughts and actions today. I choose authentic mind."

You may want to take some notes down in your phone or in your journal about what you have observed in yourself today. What actions have you taken today that were based on your *anxious mind?* What were your *anxious* thoughts today? How have you reacted to everyday things? Did any conflict arise? What has your outlook been today?

Nighttime Exercise:

If you had a chance to record some of your observations today, add to that list now. It's imperative that you reflect on these things daily by writing them down and recording them on either your phone or journal. I like a journal because there are no distractions, but do what works for you. Answer any questions you haven't answered yet from the midday exercise. You are taking an inventory here. Beside each observation, I now want you to write a new and unique reaction or thought that you normally wouldn't have considered. This new thought must come from the *authentic mind.* An example is, "A customer screamed at me today and I rolled my eyes and walked away. I stewed over it for hours, feeling angry and regretful that I didn't respond back." Your *authentic mind* reaction could be, "I walked away and went into the bathroom and let out my frustration by air punching (love air punching!). I then took some deep breaths and hoped she would have a better day today, she was obviously stressed."

Now, brace yourself, some of the *authentic mind* reactions that you record might seem a bit outlandish to you right now. That's OK and totally normal. It takes time for you to recognize your *authentic mind* as truth and *anxious mind* as a lie. Give your mind and body time to catch up. We want to write down alternate reactions that come from our *authentic mind*, not our anxious, angry, or fearful mind. Remember, we can all benefit from this exercise and we all need redirection daily no matter how long we have been recovered from our anxiety or mental illness.

Close with a Prayer:

"Thank you for showing me my anxious thoughts and actions today. I will now be aware of them for the next ten-day cycle and consistently shift from anxious to authentic thoughts. Help me to notice the moments in which I need that shift. I surrender this process to you, knowing that I will be shown what I need to see in the most perfect time. Amen."

Day Two: Self Love Day

Today's Affirmation:
"I love and keep promises to myself today. I am powerful and I
am strong."

I spoke a little bit about self-love in the book, but want to really emphasize the importance of it today. Today is about making a choice to love yourself and to commit to this change so you know you are worthy of recovery and healing. We are keeping promises we've made to ourselves today. Sometimes we are resistant and skeptical of healing from our anxiety and mental illness. We can't imagine how simple solutions we've had within us all along could possibly heal this debilitating fear we feel daily. Appreciate and love your natural self today. Appreciate and love the way your unique mind works. Observe your unique gifts. Don't forget, self-love is unconditional. We may have experienced conditional love in the past from our families or other significant relationships, but that is not what we model our self-love after. In fact, this is not how we model any form of love after. Love is unconditional.

Morning Exercise:

1. Meditate: Be totally still and don't let any body part move. Close your eyes and breathe deep slow breaths. You can mentally repeat this mantra or say it aloud,

   "I love you. You are safe. I love you. You are safe."

As you take long inhales and long slow exhales, say the mantra in your mind or aloud to the rhythm of the breath. Don't worry if your thoughts drift, just come back to the mantra. Do this for 5-10 mins. Let your body go a little limp at the end and take a big sigh of relief.

2. Say this morning's affirmation out loud with your hand placed on your heart:

"I love and accept myself. I am a gift to the world. My mind is unique and my thoughts are of love. I use my authentic mind to think of all my attributes today. I use my authentic mind to think of all the reasons why I am so strong today. I am worthy of the life I desire. I enjoy myself. Others' opinions of me are none of my business. I will leave it to them because I truly don't care. I know in my heart that I am a person of love. I bring joy to myself and others. I am inspiring, and I am strong!"

Now gently smile to yourself. Take a deep breath in and a calming breath out.

3. Don't forget to do a daily check in with yourself regarding your technology use. Make one subtle change today.

Midday Exercise:

Around noon or lunchtime, take a minute to check in with yourself, put your hand to your heart, close your eyes and say today's mantra three times.

Today's affirmation to put in your phone and repeat all day long:
"I love and keep promises to myself today. I am powerful and strong."

Take some notes in your phone or journal about the good and positive things you do today. Write down things you like about yourself, your body, and personality. Stay aware of these things all day. Also, brainstorm and prepare an act of self-care that you will do for yourself tonight.

Nighttime Exercise:

If you had a chance to record some of your observations today, add to that list now. Answer any questions you haven't answered yet from the midday exercise. After you list everything you love about yourself and some examples of those in which you observed today, I want you to partake in some form of self-care tonight. Whatever it is that you do, you must consciously make it about self-love.

Some examples of this may be:

- taking a bath
- reading a book
- getting a massage
- doing some calming stretches
- creating something like a poem, painting, or a craft
- cooking a nice meal for yourself and eating slowly and consciously, enjoying every flavor

Just make sure it's something you truly enjoy doing. Acts of self-care are only meant to be things that you enjoy. This is not the time to force yourself to do something you don't 100% enjoy.

Also, if you're not used to forms of self-care, it may feel odd for you at first and don't panic if you feel like you're not fully present. Trust me, the ability to enjoy things like self-care can take practice for some people, but it will feel so naturally enjoyable the more you reprogram your mind.

Finally: Journal about how it felt to focus on how much you love yourself today. Did it feel odd? Did it feel wrong or did it feel normal? Are you resistant to self-care and self-love? Do you have any limiting beliefs around self-love? After your journal entry, write:

"I love and forgive myself for any limiting beliefs I have around self-care and self-love."

Day Three: Dreams and Desires Day

Today's Affirmation:
"Today, I'm giving my dreams power. There are no limitations to my dreams. I am worthy."

Today, we focus only on our dreams and desires. This is such a fun day! This is the day when you allow yourself to dream big dreams for yourself. I believe that our desires were placed within our hearts for a reason, so today we honor them. We give those desires and dreams power today, and we look to be inspired today. We are going to get genuinely excited about our lives today.

Today, you're going to talk about your dreams as though they are really going to happen. Today, open your mind to your dreams. They are your dreams for a reason. Talk about your dreams as if they are real and happening to you now. How excited would you be? What feelings and emotions would come over you? One thing you need to do in order for your dreams to come true is to give them power. We too often give negative things so much power over our lives. Enough of that now. Let's give our dreams power today!

Morning Exercise:

1. Meditate: Be totally still and don't let any body part move. Close your eyes and breathe deep slow breaths. You can mentally repeat this mantra or say it aloud,

   "I give my dreams and desires power."

Don't worry if your thoughts drift, just come back to the mantra. Do this for 5-10 mins. Let your body go a little limp at the end and take a big sigh of relief.

2. Say this morning's prayer out loud:

"Guide me today to become clear on what my heart wants. Sometimes I am so distracted by my anxiety that I don't even really know what I want. I don't often give my dreams and desires the power they deserve because I don't truly believe I am worthy of them. Help me to see how much I deserve to live my dreams out today. Help me to have goals and to visualize my dreams becoming reality. Help me to understand the emotions I should feel when thinking of my dreams and desires, are pure joy and excitement. Help me discover who I am and what my true desires are. Help me see beyond logic today and only stay within my dreams. Amen."

3. Don't forget to do a daily check in with yourself regarding your technology use. Make one subtle change today.

Midday Exercise:

Around noon or lunchtime, take a minute to check in with yourself, put your hand to your heart, close your eyes and say today's mantra three times.

Today's affirmation to put in your phone and repeat all day long: "Today, I'm giving my dreams power. There are no limitations to my dreams. I am worthy."

Take some notes down in your phone or journal about things that come up for you when you think about your dreams. Write down both your dreams and any limiting beliefs or thoughts that come up for you. Often, we feel as though we are undeserving or unworthy of making our dreams become a reality. Maybe we think we would be leaving someone behind or that we don't have the right to be happy. Explore this in your journal.

Nighttime Exercise:

Finish your journaling and list from your midday exercise during this time. When you are doing this, think also about what gets you genuinely excited to dream. These dreams may involve travel, vacations, career, finances and relationships. Dream big! Nothing is unrealistic or off the table here. I also want you to think about the things you desire. Some things you desire may be more time with friends and family, or more time for peace and relaxation.

Some of my dreams and desires are:

- wanting to visit Ireland
- working on a movie set
- going to Las Vegas again with all my friends
- having the financial abundance I've always wanted
- living in LA for a few months every year
- meeting some of my clients and amazing people in my field in person
- eating fancy dinners at this hotel in Niagara

Some people may think my dreams are unrealistic and I couldn't care a less. Neither should you.

Tonight is all about holding your dreams close to your heart.

Day Four: Change Your Expectations Day

Today's Affirmation:
"I am excited to see how life surprises me when I
change my expectations today."

We touch a little on releasing and changing expectations in the book, but today we practice it. This practice is intensively eye-opening and will undoubtedly supply you with plenty of "AHA" moments throughout the day. We all have expectations, constantly. Anxiety sufferers have more. We often place those expectations on ourselves more than on anyone else. We have incredibly high expectations of ourselves and when we don't live up to them, we are so hard on ourselves. Today will open your eyes to the ways in which you put expectations on yourself and others.

These expectations are sneaky and we often don't even notice them. For instance, you may expect your partner to clean up after themselves and when they don't, you get super ticked off. Or maybe you expect yourself to eat better, exercise more, or even sleep longer. Today is the day we bring these expectations to light and also choose to release them. We are challenging those expectations today, so pay close attention. These expectations don't always have to involve people either. Perhaps you have an expectation of the weather or about how your day at work will go. We have imaginative minds, so we are always picturing how things will go. Even right now, I'm picturing how my walk down the street will go. I expect it to be nice and warm outside and I expect that I won't run into anyone that I know because I'm wearing a crazy outfit. When you surrender those expectations and release them, you often get pleasantly surprised by life. So, let's get to work at dropping as many expectations as we can today.

Hint: If you find yourself saying or thinking the word "should" a lot, that's a good indication of expectation.

Morning Exercise:

1. Meditate: Be totally still and don't let any body part move. Close your eyes and breathe deep slow breaths. You can mentally repeat this mantra or say it aloud,

    "I release expectations."

    Don't worry if your thoughts drift, just come back to the mantra. Do this for 5-10 mins. Let your body go a little limp at the end and take a big sigh of relief.

2. Take out your journal and list your expectations for the next few hours. What would really set you off if it didn't work out the way you expected it to? What do you expect from the people you interact with today? Do you expect them to be in a certain mood? Do you expect them to act a certain way? How will you react if they don't? This is not a time to judge yourself or others. Remember that everyone is doing the best they can do and the best way to heal is to practice forgiveness over and over again. This forgiveness applies to both yourself and others.

3. Say this morning's affirmation out loud with your hand placed upon your heart:

   "Today I observe my expectations. I am willing to release and surrender my expectations, knowing that if things don't work out the way I expected them to, that it's ok. It's ok because everything happens for a reason. I release the need to control areas of my life. I release the immense pressure I put on myself today. Even if it's just for today, I choose thoughts of the authentic mind. I allow life to surprise me today by releasing my expectations of how things 'should' go."

4. Don't forget to do a daily check in with yourself regarding your technology use. Make one subtle change today.

Midday Exercise:

Around noon or lunchtime, take a minute to check in with yourself, put your hand to your heart, close your eyes and say today's mantra three times.

Today's affirmation to put in your phone and repeat all day long:
"I am excited to see how life surprises me when I change my expectations today.'

Take some notes in your phone or journal about how your day has panned out so far. Reflect on your morning expectations. What expectations worked out? What happened that didn't match up with your expectations from this morning? How did you react?

Nighttime Exercise:

Take out your journal. How did you feel doing this activity today? What did you notice about your expectations of others, of yourself, and of outside factors like the weather? Did you have any eye-opening moments today? What expectations would be helpful to practice releasing? Were you pleasantly surprised after releasing your expectations today? How hard were you on yourself and on others? Take this opportunity now to write about forgiveness. I want you to just write out who you need to forgive for not meeting your expectations today. Do you need to forgive yourself too? Take this time to journal out forgiveness.

Day Five: Gratitude Day

Today's Affirmation:
"I focus only on unconditional gratitude today and I
appreciate my unique mind."

Gratitude extinguishes fear and anxiety. When we can learn to see the true value in gratitude and the immense change it brings to our lives, we can benefit from its impacts. Practicing gratitude will only bring you further in your life and recovery. Like everything, we must practice it to excel at it. The *anxious mind* wants to put gratitude on the back burner. The *authentic mind* wants to glorify gratitude and appreciates the benefits it brings us. *Authentic mind* amplifies the messages of gratitude. Today, we focus on this beautiful practice and understand that *authentic mind* always moves easily and naturally towards being grateful.

Morning Exercise:

1. Meditate: Be totally still and don't let any body part move. Close your eyes and breathe deep slow breaths. You can mentally repeat this mantra or say it aloud,

   "I am grateful. I am blessed."

Don't worry if your thoughts drift, just come back to the mantra. Do this for 5-10 mins. Let your body go a little limp at the end and take a big sigh of relief.

2. Say this morning's prayer out loud:

   "Guide me today to see gratitude. Open my eyes so that I can see how fortunate I truly am. Despite what is going right or wrong in my life, help me to see there are always many things to be grateful for. Help me to notice the small things today. Guide me today to see all the reasons for which I am grateful for my anxiety. Show me the ways in which it has changed my life for the better. Help me to be in a state of calm and gratitude. Amen."

3. Take a moment this morning to pull out your journal. I want you to write a gratitude list. A gratitude list is one of my favorite tools for healing. I keep one all the time and enjoy adding to it. They are also beautiful things to open up and reflect on when you're having an anxious moment or are stuck in circular thinking. This list is something I want you to begin this morning and continue throughout the day. This morning, focus your gratitude list on yourself. What are you grateful for when it comes to your mind and body? What personality traits and qualities are you grateful to have? What talents and gifts are you grateful for? Dig deep here. This may be challenging, but that's okay, I guarantee you can fill pages.

4. Don't forget to do a daily check in with yourself regarding your technology use. Make one subtle change today.

Midday Exercise:

Around noon or lunchtime, take a minute to check in with yourself, put your hand to your heart, close your eyes and say today's mantra three times.

Today's affirmation to put in your phone and repeat all day long:
"I focus only on unconditional gratitude today and appreciate my unique mind."

Take some notes down in your phone or journal about things that come up for you when you think about what you are thankful for. Some suggested areas to focus on are family, friends, your home, finances and health. I can promise you, despite your current situation in life, if you dig deep you can fill in all these areas.

Nighttime Exercise:

Finish your list from your morning and midday exercises. Now that you're finished with your list, I want you to journal about your experiences with your list today. Did it come easily to you? What areas in your life do you most struggle with when it comes to gratitude? Why do you think that is? What are the benefits your anxiety or mental illness has brought to you today? What characteristics of yourself do you love that are a result of your anxiety?

Tonight, we close with another prayer before you relax for the evening.

"Thank you for my unique mind. I am grateful for the way I view the world. At times, my mind tells me lies. Thank you for helping me to see they are not the truth. Help me to return to my authentic mind and a place of gratitude. Help me to understand that living in a place of constant gratitude is where I want to be. I am grateful for my experiences, despite how difficult and dark they have been. I know that I will one day be able to use these experiences to help others and make a massive change. As I rest tonight, help me run over the reasons as to why I am grateful. Help me to gently smile to myself as I look around and see the potential that is my life. Amen."

Day Six: Restoring your Immaturity Day

Today's Affirmation:
"I honor my truth today. For it was during childhood that I
was closest to my authentic mind."

Oh, today is a fun one! I love reconnecting with the things I loved to do as a child. Anytime that I have practiced this day, it makes me happy, and that can be a challenge for someone living with a mental illness or anxiety. Life can start to lose its color and in turn, we lose our youthful joy and genuine excitement for life that we once had. Don't take life so seriously today. It's actually funny to think how much we try and control it. Laugh hard and hysterically today! Be bold with kindness today. Joke around today. Let down your walls and laugh at yourself. Today is the day to practice everything we've learned earlier in the book about embracing your immature and childlike self.

Morning Exercise:

1. I spoke about this in the intro to the 40-day program and today we are going to pull out the music. I like to make a point to find some of my favorite old songs when practicing this day. You can actually make up a playlist. Music is an incredibly healing tool and we are going to use that to our advantage. So, create a positive nostalgic playlist on your phone, or grab your favorite old CDs. The songs you choose today have to qualify in three ways: they must be from your childhood, you must have positive associations with them, and they can't be songs

you listen to regularly. If you are on your second, third or fourth round of these 10 days, switch up your playlist a bit every week. This MUST be a fun experience, so shock your *anxious mind* and switch the songs up. Organize that song list this morning and make sure you listen all day long.

2. Choose one or several activities today that will embrace your childlike self. Write these down in your journal. These can simply just be ideas that you record, but make sure to partake in at least one of them today. The goal is to get you nostalgic in a positive way. We want to reconnect with that childlike self that we once were but have now forgotten. That person is still inside of you. They never left. Today we embrace that.

3. Meditate: Be totally still and don't let any body part move. Close your eyes and breathe deep slow breaths. You can mentally repeat this mantra or say it aloud, as if you are saying it to a younger version of yourself:

    "I love you. You are safe. I love you. You are safe."

    As you take long inhales and long slow exhales, say the mantra in your mind or aloud to the rhythm of the breath. Do this for 5-10 mins. Don't worry if your thoughts drift, just come back to the mantra. Let your body go a little limp at the end and take a big sigh of relief.

4. Say this morning's prayer out loud:

    "I pray to see the world through a child's eyes today. It was when I was a child that I was closer to being my true self. Help me to bring my walls

down and love unconditionally today. The world around me is so magical. Help me to understand that seeing the world through the eyes of a child, with all its beauty, is possible for me as an adult too. Help me to understand that my childhood dreams do not have to die just because I am of a certain age. Today, help me to restore my immaturity. Amen."

5. Don't forget to do a daily check in with yourself regarding your technology use. Make one subtle change today.

Midday Exercise:

Around noon or lunchtime, take a minute to check in with yourself, put your hand to your heart, close your eyes and say today's mantra three times.

Today's affirmation to put in your phone and repeat all day long:
"I honor my truth today. For it was during childhood that I was closest to my authentic mind."

Take some notes in your phone or journal regarding your happiest childhood memories. What were you doing? Who were you spending your time with? How did you feel? How can you reconnect with those enjoying activities and memories today as an adult? (Remember, we are not talking about reliving or re-creating these memories because that can often be challenging and not very fruitful.) We are simply getting excited here and exploring what we can do to bring those feelings back into our daily lives. Now, record what you have done so far today to embrace your immaturity. Your childlike self. How did it make you feel? Describe what you did.

Nighttime Exercise:

Take out your journal and add to the midday journal entry here. Now we are going to explore even further. Let's talk about places. Where are your places of joy? Do you have some unconventional ones? Tonight's exercise is a fun one. The weirder, the better! I personally love coffee shops (I don't drink coffee), the smell of Italian restaurants, and ice cream shops. I love taking drives at night and could do that for hours. Oh yeah, and I love walking around hotels and smelling the pool area. Don't judge!

We close by repeating this morning's meditation with a visualization. Those places you just journaled about, I want you to bring into your meditation tonight. I want you to go into an intense visualization of those places. I want you to see yourself enjoying these places today, as an adult. As you visualize, I want you to picture your adult-self and your child-self having fun and enjoying these places together. You act like each other's best friend, laughing and joking with one another. This powerful visualization will help to bring calm into your night.

Day Seven: Marveling Day

Today's Affirmation:
"I live today in awe of the beauty around me. I smell, feel,
hear, taste and see life today."

Today is about being in this moment right here. It's funny because it's actually something I've always hated hearing. I would absolutely loath when someone would tell me to "live in the moment." I never knew how the hell I was supposed to do that with my severe obsessive thoughts. I didn't even know what it meant to "live in the moment." The further along I got in my healing process, the more I understood what it meant, what it entailed, and how it felt. I want to simplify "living in the moment," for people with anxiety and mental illness. Living in the moment comes with consistency. We must practice it. That's why I always got so frustrated when someone would just casually suggest it. I had no idea where to start. One practice that I love to do that brings me right to the moment is what I call "marveling." My marveling practice is to simply stop and look around at my surroundings. I want you to marvel at the beauty around you. Stare with an open mouth at the world. Be aware of the hidden beauty in it all. Look at things with gratitude and for the people and things you have. Remember there is beauty in everything, and today's goal is to find it. I want you to take it all in today. Look around and memorize every beautiful detail. Today is a wonderful opportunity to be highly aware of all of your senses. You will have even more heightened senses of smell, sight, touch, sound and taste today. Breathe in gratitude. Taste it, feel it, hear it, smell it and touch it.

Be thankful for your senses today. If you are missing or have one weak sense, be grateful for the ones that you do have. Our senses provide so much pleasure in our day-to-day lives. I'm sorry, but there's nothing better than tasting birthday cake ice cream. There's also nothing better than feeling the love a hug can provide. So be thankful for your senses today. It's something we take for granted far too often.

As said earlier in "The Five Senses of Peace," as anxiety sufferers, we have heightened senses and we can use this to our advantage and understand that, like everything, it's not a curse. It's a gift we can use by stopping and closing our eyes outside and truly feeling all the sensations of nature around us, even if we live in the city. We can see the beauty in things that other people may not.

Like the final step in "The Five Senses," we live out today in a place of childlike wonder and curiosity. We live today in gratitude for the beauty that surrounds us. Walk around slowly today, as if you were walking in water. Touch leaves and let your fingers linger on them. Close your eyes, smell, and be observant in gratitude. The world around us is always beautiful. It just depends on whether we're noticing it or not. There are so many things to be appreciated in the world, but we tend not to even notice them. Something as simple as watching a mother care for her little child or someone opening the door for an elderly person can be overlooked so easily. Take a moment today to look around you. Try and find something beautiful that you can appreciate and would typically walk right past. It's vital to our joy and happiness that we start noticing these things and appreciating them.

Morning Exercise:

1. Meditate: Be totally still and don't let any body part move. Close your eyes and breathe deep, slow breaths. You can mentally repeat this mantra or say it aloud,

   "I am curious about the world around me."

   Don't worry if your thoughts drift, just come back to the mantra. Do this for 5-10 mins. Let your body go a little limp at the end and take a big sigh of relief.

2. Say this morning's affirmation out loud:

   "The world around me is a place of wonder and beauty. I connect with my five heightened senses today and look at them as the gift that they are. I understand that not everyone in this world experiences the five senses. Even if one of my senses is weak or gone, I appreciate the beauty and strength of the senses that I do have. I am excited for the day ahead and to record the beauty I will discover today."

3. Don't forget to do a daily check in with yourself regarding your technology use. Make one subtle change today.

Midday Exercise:

Around noon or lunchtime, take a minute to check in with yourself, put your hand to your heart, close your eyes and say today's mantra three times.

Today's affirmation to put in your phone and repeat all day long:
"I live today in awe of the beauty around me. I smell, feel, hear,
taste and see life today."

Take some notes in your phone or journal about things that are beautiful around you today. Think of unconventional things. Have fun with this. Dig deeper than just the surface. Notice the vibrant color of the fruit you have for lunch. Take a moment and smell it before you eat it. Take a minute to stare at its details. Record some of these moments in your journal today.

Nighttime Exercise:

Finish your list up from your morning and midday exercises. Now that you're finished with your list, I want you to journal about your experiences with your list today. Did it come easily to you? What senses are you grateful for? What did you notice in your mood and outlook when you started this practice today?

Tonight we close by repeating this morning's meditation and mantra again. During this meditation, visualize and re-live some of the moments of conventional and unconventional beauty in the world around you that you experienced today. Visualize the things you recorded and go back into those moments of "awe" and wonder.

Day Eight: Change Your Routine Day

Today's Affirmation:
"I am safe to change up a routine today. I choose to take
the next steps to heal. It is my time now."

Even if it's just for one day, it's important to switch up your routines. Routines can make or break our recovery and can support or hinder our mindset journey. We all have habits and routines; it's whether or not they are helpful to us that truly matters. Some of us have obsessive thoughts or actions around our routines. We are convinced that if we don't adhere to our strict rules, chaos will ensue. It's important to weaken some of the rules we have around our routines. When we adhere to such restrictions around our days, there leaves no wiggle room to make way for other, more beneficial things to come through. For example, when I was a smoker, I used to have a cigarette as soon as I woke up. When I decided that I wanted to eventually quit, I started slowly switching up my routines with my cigarettes. Instead of having one as soon as I woke up, I delayed having it for 30 minutes. It was a small change, but it tricked my *anxious mind* and started to strengthen my *authentic.* I did that every day for a few months, never sticking to my routines with the cigarettes. As the months went on, I had no smoking patterns left. The routines were all over the place. Now, today doesn't have to just be about negative patterns and routines in your day. You're simply challenging your daily routine, in turn weakening the *anxious mind* by proving you don't NEED to stick to your patterns. The *anxious mind* thrives on patterns and routines and those things can keep us stuck, without us even knowing it. Perhaps you watch the same TV show every day during breakfast, or you need to have a coffee before being able to function. Today, we choose a routine to switch up! Be grateful for today, for it is a huge step in your recovery journey.

Morning Exercise:

1. Meditate: Be totally still and don't let any body part move. Close your eyes and breathe deep slow breaths. You can mentally repeat this mantra or say it aloud,

"I change routines in love. I am safe."

Don't worry if your thoughts drift, just come back to the mantra. Do this for 5-10 mins. Let your body go a little limp at the end and take a big sigh of relief.

2. Taking out your journal right now, I want you to list your daily routines that make you feel safe. Some examples of these may be: I wake up and directly go take my morning vitamins, or I get out of bed and jump in the shower. Now, rate these routines as 1 to 10 in how much anxiety it would bring you to drop them or change them. Number 1 being no stress, and number 10 being intense stress. Next, I want you to circle one thing you will switch up today. If this is your first round of the ten days, I want you to start out with something that you marked in between the numbers of 1-4. You can increase the challenges as the 40 days go on. Just go with whatever feels OK

and natural to you. Don't force yourself to change something marked as a 10 that you're not ready to try. Be kind to yourself.

3. Say this morning's affirmation out loud with your hand placed upon your heart:

"Today I switch things up. Even if it's just for one day. I am committed to changing at least one routine today. I know that in the past, my routines have been my safety. In a world and in a mind in which I don't feel safe in, my routines are something I can control. I release the need to control today, knowing that I am safe without my routines. I know that these routines have served me well in the past, but I no longer need them anymore. I thank my routines for what they provided for me when I needed them the most, but I now release the power they have over me."

4. Don't forget to do a daily check in with yourself regarding your technology use. Make one subtle change today.

Midday Exercise:

Around noon or lunchtime, take a minute to check in with yourself, put your hand to your heart, close your eyes and say today's mantra three times.

Today's affirmation to put in your phone and repeat all day long:
"I am safe to change up a routine today. I choose to take the next steps to heal. It is my time now."

Take some notes in your phone or journal about feelings that come up for you when you changed up your routine from this morning. If you haven't done it yet, write about how you feel about doing it.

Nighttime Exercise:

Taking out your list from this morning, I want you to write beside or below each routine, a small thing you can do to change it. If it was that you have to shower as soon as you wake up, your response to that can be to shower 15 mins later than normal or take vitamins 15 mins later than normal. Then, I want you to write a little more of an intense challenge next to each one. With the examples used above, it could be: "Skip my shower or skip my vitamins altogether." These are not things you need to do, although you may choose to try them at some point. The point of this exercise is just to gently get you thinking and reflecting on your routines during the day.

In your journal, you are now to write on this subject: Which routines support you in your recovery from anxiety? Which routines do you think hinder you? How did you feel challenging those routines today? Were you surprised at all by the work you did today?

Day Nine: Pay it Forward Day

Today's Affirmation:
"Today I will do good deeds, asking for nothing in return. I give out
kindness freely today and am excited to make someone's day."

One of the most important parts of recovery and healing is the ability to spread light and joy to others. Today is the day to pay it forward and help others out. We all know what it's like to feel lonely and as though no one cares. Today we practice spreading joy to others, despite where we are at. We put aside our own anxieties and focus on other people today. This is not to say that we are not important. In fact, after reading this book, we are now starting to understand how important we really are. Hopefully, by now, you understand you don't need other people in order for you to heal. You can heal, and you've had the power to heal all along. We can appreciate our anxiety for what it has done for us in the past, for we needed it for survival. Now, we can gently dismiss it and tell it we don't need it anymore. However, there are still people out there suffering that don't have this information. Maybe you pass a copy of this book to a friend or family member today to pay it forward. Perhaps you do something as simple as pay for someone's coffee or send a simple text telling someone you are thinking about them and love and appreciate them. You don't need to overwhelm yourself here.

Today is all about following your heart. Don't force it, let it come naturally. Understand other people and know that no matter how people act, everyone has their own battles they are fighting.

Maybe paying it forward for you simply means not flipping someone the bird if they cut you off on the highway, understanding that they may be having a bad day. Don't drain yourself or burn yourself out today. I know it's common amongst anxiety sufferers to burn out trying to help others, and that is NOT what today is about. Today is about doing good things in excitement and in joy.

Don't forget to get creative with how to pay it forward. Take the opportunity this morning to come up with some fun and different ways to help others or be kind. Sometimes I like to just hand strangers money. It's hilarious to see their reactions, but a pretty cool social experiment. I like to really watch people and decide to perhaps "tip" the gas station attendant $50.00 and just watch the reaction. I would do this even when I was broke because I knew what it meant to them. Keep in mind, you may not get anything back in return today. Society is not really used to people giving out kindness for free these days. You may get some odd reactions, but know that you're doing this from the goodness of your own heart. You're not doing this for recognition. You're not doing it to be thanked or even care or expect anyone to thank you. You are just doing good for the sake of doing good.

Morning Exercise:

1. Meditate: Be totally still and don't let any body part move. Close your eyes and breathe deep slow breaths. You can mentally repeat this mantra or say it aloud,

"I am excited to make someone's day today."

Don't worry if your thoughts drift, just come back to the mantra. Do it for 5-10 mins. Let your body go a little limp at the end and take a big sigh of relief.

2. Take out your journal and brainstorm some creative ways in which you can help or pay it forward today.

3. Say this morning's affirmation out loud with your hand placed upon your heart:

"Today is an exciting day for me. Today I am going to pay it forward in cool and creative ways. I can start small and work my way up. I don't expect a thank you today. That is not why I am doing this. Today I look for opportunities to do good. I watch out for them in excitement. Helping others is a way in which my recovery can make a difference. One day, I hope to help someone else on their journey to recovery. I am excited at the thought of helping and connecting to other people because that is the essence of life."

4. Don't forget to do a daily check in with yourself regarding your technology use. Make one subtle change today.

Midday Exercise:

Around noon or lunchtime, take a minute to check in with yourself, put your hand to your heart, close your eyes and say today's mantra three times.

Today's affirmation to put in your phone and repeat all day long:
"Today I will do good deeds, asking for nothing in return. I give out kindness freely today and am excited to make someone's day."

Take some notes in your phone or journal about how you have made an effort to help someone or pay it forward so far. This can be holding the door for someone or smiling at a passerby. Is there anything that holds you back? Why do you think that is? Journal on forgiving any hesitations you may have.

Nighttime Exercise:

Take out your list from today, and add onto it. Journal about the reactions you got from others and how you felt about what you did today. If you received no reactions, write in your journal about how good it feels to do good without the need for a thank you or acknowledgment.

Day Ten: Victory Day

Today's Affirmation:
"I celebrate my commitment to change today. I'm so
damn proud of myself today."

Today is the day to acknowledge yourself for all of your very hard work. The fact that you're showing up, doing the work, and committing to yourself is more outstanding than you know. Today, we tune into our victories. Today we are proud of ourselves. Today we understand that we need to look within for the answers and make an unwavering commitment to change. If we don't change, nothing else will either. Your choices are the root of everything in your life, including your thoughts. You can always choose *authentic mind* over *anxious*, it just depends on how committed you are to the process. Today you celebrate that commitment.

Morning Exercise:

1. Meditate: Be totally still and don't let any body part move. Close your eyes and breathe deep slow breaths. You can mentally repeat this mantra or say it aloud,

    "I am victorious. I am proud."

    Don't worry if your thoughts drift, just come back to the mantra. Do this for 5-10 mins. Let your body go a little limp at the end and take a big sigh of relief.

2. This morning I want you to listen to 10 minutes of personal development. This can be audios or videos of some of your favorite motivational speakers or teachers. If you don't have

any favorites, take time now to research some videos. Listen to them this morning while you sit or while you get ready for your day. It's okay if it's on in the background; just make sure it's on. Today you're giving yourself a break. You've worked really hard.

3. Don't forget to do a daily check in with yourself regarding your technology use. Make one subtle change today.

Midday Exercise:

Around noon or lunchtime, take a minute to check in with yourself, put your hand to your heart, close your eyes and say today's mantra three times.

Today's affirmation to put in your phone and repeat all day long:
"I celebrate my commitment to change today. I'm so damn proud of myself today."

Take some notes in your phone or journal about your progress. What have you found to be easy during this program? What have you found challenging? What have been some of your victories these past ten days? How have you detoxed from technology this week? How has it felt?

Nighttime Exercise:

Take out your journal and add onto your midday exercise. You can go back and reflect in your journal on your successes. At the bottom of the page write and say aloud, "I am proud of myself for showing up to do this work. I am healing and it was easier than I thought."

Chapter 23
So, Now What?

So you have read the book, done the 40-day program and are probably thinking, now what? Well, this final chapter has been designed to answer that exact question. This book is a tool to keep forever. When you go on vacation or when you have something stressful approaching, reach for this book. I designed this book to be read over again. As you've learned throughout the book, the *anxious mind* is powerful because we have been programmed to choose those thoughts over *authentic* ones. We must overcome the thoughts within the mind with consistency. This is a lifelong journey. You may have moments in a few years from now that may trigger some anxiety again. That's okay. You know what to do now if that happens. You are prepared, so it's not scary anymore. The answers are in this book. Re-do the 40-day program, re-read the book, and re-write your journal entries. We are always growing and evolving, taking new things we have learned and applying them to live better lives. We are moving forward and doing better. Be patient with yourself, but keep promises to yourself as well by staying on top of your recovery every single day. When you start feeling better, you need to work just as hard every single day as a preventative measure.

Out of any resources that we possess, there is one that is the most valuable, non-renewable, and undervalued, which is time.

Many of you feel as though your anxiety and mental illness has robbed you of so much time. I can completely relate to that and it used to make my anxiety worse when I thought about wasting any more of my precious life. These hard-earned lessons that I have learned have turned my life into one that I couldn't ever have dreamed of before. However, learning these lessons cost me so much of that precious time. I want more for you.

That *anxious* thought of wasted time used to give me an ache every night before I went to bed. I knew I needed to heal and heal fast. That's when I decided to make the investment in myself and also for my loved ones and friends around me. I no longer wanted to feel as if I were wasting anymore time, so I tried coaching. Coaching gave me the support I so desperately needed. It helped me not feel alone in my struggle anymore. I remember actually emailing my coach before getting on an airplane during a panic attack. She was able to quickly shift my mind, and I was able to face one of my biggest fears successfully.

That's what coaching does. It helps you to shift from *anxious* to *authentic mind* when you may otherwise not be as strong on your own. It helps train the brain until it becomes natural, but it lends you the constant support you have longed for. It provides clarity in things you are doubtful about. Coaching cannot replace therapy and vice versa, but the combination of the two compliments one another in so many ways. I did both and preferred the coaching. It provided me with someone who had been where I had been and knew how to guide me out. The progress was amazing too. I am convinced that it accelerated ten years in my recovery process in only six months. Sure, I could have done it on my own. I could've toughed it out, tried and failed and tried again until I got it. I was determined, as I know you are, and I would've eventually figured it out. However, time was precious to me. How many vacations would have been ruined? How many nights of sleep would I have lost? How many important events with friends and family would I have opted out of? How much of my time would I have squandered? My time was too important to me, and the support was too.

It was also so important for me to find the right person. A coach who really understood me and got what I was going through. When I found my coach and heard parts of her story, her journey, and her struggles, I knew she was the one to help me. She related to my hardships. She had been through it too. The fact that she had been where I had been and overcome it was inspiring to me. It gave me hope. She became a coach and a mentor to me. I learned what she learned along her path and it helped me to level up much faster than I ever would have on my own.

Investing in yourself is something you can't put a price on. When you invest in yourself and in your recovery, you become a better father, mother, husband, wife, daughter and son. You accelerate more in your career and finances and end up getting your investment back tenfold. I have invested in so many different personal development products and coaching over the years and don't regret a single one of them. Once you get your anxiety to a place of ease and recovery, you can start to focus on advancing in other areas of your life too. You can start focusing on your finances and living out your dreams. You can focus on your career or family and start to truly see how happy you can be in all areas of your life.

This is where personal development is the key. Courses, books, audios and coaching can all help you to up-level in your life. The stigma of anxiety and mental illness will no longer exist in your mind and you will be ready to help others and move on in big, massive ways. Get excited for the potential you have. This is the only life we get. Don't waste it by letting fear hold you back. Don't listen to the lies of the *anxious mind*. You can start over at any age. You can decide to up level in your life anytime you want.

Don't forget that you have the information you need to move forward. Stand strong in your recovery. Once the anxiety is out of the way, you will have the ability to tackle so much more to achieve greatness and to help others. You no longer have to give the *anxious mind* power; it's all lies.

Lies your mind tells you.

Made in the USA
Lexington, KY
18 February 2018